2004 POETR

ONCE UPON A RHYME

IMAGINATION FOR
A NEW GENERATION

North Yorkshire
Edited by Chris Hallam

 Young**Writers**

First published in Great Britain in 2004 by:
Young Writers
Remus House
Coltsfoot Drive
Peterborough
PE2 9JX
Telephone: 01733 890066
Website: www.youngwriters.co.uk

SB ISBN 1 84460 480 2

Foreword

Young Writers was established in 1991 and has been passionately devoted to the promotion of reading and writing in children and young adults ever since. The quest continues today. Young Writers remains as committed to engendering the fostering of burgeoning poetic and literary talent as ever.

This year's Young Writers competition has proven as vibrant and dynamic as ever and we are delighted to present a showcase of the best poetry from across the UK. Each poem has been carefully selected from a wealth of *Once Upon A Rhyme* entries before ultimately being published in this, our twelfth primary school poetry series.

Once again, we have been supremely impressed by the overall high quality of the entries we have received. The imagination, energy and creativity which has gone into each young writer's entry made choosing the best poems a challenging and often difficult but ultimately hugely rewarding task - the general high standard of the work submitted amply vindicating this opportunity to bring their poetry to a larger appreciative audience.

We sincerely hope you are pleased with our final selection and that you will enjoy *Once Upon A Rhyme North Yorkshire* for many years to come.

Contents

Daniel Williams (9)   14
Ross Thwaites (7)   14

Baldersby St James CE Primary School
Libby Lang-Burns (7)   14
Gilly Thorne (8)   15
Jade Dunn (8)   15
Ben Hunt (9)   15
Megan Kettlewell (9)   16
Katie Utley (8)   16

Birstwith CE Primary School
Alexandra Groom (9)   16
Jessica Umpleby (10)   17
Jacob Eastland (10)   17
Kaya Oldaker (10)   18
Kate Rollerson (9)   18
Adam Willford (11)   19
Helen Hovell (10)   19
Hayley Metcalfe (10)   20
Kate Robinson (10)   21
Emma Waddington (10)   22
Mark Foster (11)   22
Cleone Pardoe (10)   23
Josie Caven (10)   24
Megan Caven (10)   25
Sophie Hodgson (11)   26
Ehlana Hodgson (11)   27
Emma Groom (9)   27
Emily Reynard (10)   28

Carnagill County Primary School
Arron Gent (9)   28
Jasmine Lindsey (10)   29

Dishforth Airfield Community Primary School
Daniel Kenny (11)   29
Alexandra Quinn (10)   30
Steven Stewart (10)   31
Jennifer McMillan (11)   31

Foston CE Primary School

Jamie Noble (9)	31
Jessica Woardby (9)	32
Lianne Noble (11)	32

Hambleton CE Primary School

Megan Bell (11)	33
Anna Wynne (10)	34
Emily Barlow (10)	35
Emma Pendlebury (9)	36
Laura Perry (9)	37
Mark Pooleman (10)	38
Thea Muscroft (10)	38
Lauren Dunwell (9)	39
Rachel Cullen (9)	39
Emily Davies (9)	40

Hookstone Chase CP School

Joanna Hopkinson (10)	40
Sophie Sadler (9)	41
Amy Rose Humphrey (8)	41
Adam Hodgson (11)	41
Mia Kilpatrick (11)	42
Olivia Connolly (8)	42
Martin Priestley (11)	43
Chloë Ince-Knight (11)	43
Joanne Allcock (11)	44
Megan Davies (10)	44
Mathew Wills (10)	45
Amie Tipling (11)	45
Tom Flynn (11)	45
Melanie Saville (11)	46
Rebecca Leigh (11)	46
Katie Fenn (9)	46
Almasa Pašalic (10)	47
Robert Ellis (11)	47
Kirsty Hunter (11)	48
Gabriella Cooper (10)	48
Brynmor Powell (10)	49
Jonny Allan (10)	49
Jodie McCarthy (10)	49

Bethany Balla (10)   50
Caitlin Chang (10)   50
Romy Jade Anderson (10)   51
Georgina Smith (10)   51
Katie Head (9)   52
Katy Walters (10)   52
Oliver Chapman (9)   52
Elliott Gray (10)   53

Ingleby Arncliffe CE Primary School

Millie Sanderson (10)   53
Hannah Miles (10)   54
Ben Stephenson (11)   54
Sachin Kumarendran (9)   55
Emma Barlow (10)   55
David Carr (10)   55
Mark Libby (9)   56
Rebecca Marsden (10)   56
Charity Cornforth (9)   57
Emily Kitching (9)   57

Longman's Hill CP School

Joshua Meyer (10)   58
Sam Gill (10)   58
Joshua Oliver (11)   59
Alice Priddy (10)   60
Rebecca Meir (10)   61
Emma Noble (10)   61
Lauren Gouldsbrough (10)   62
Lauren Darley (10)   63
Amy Richardson (10)   64
Jordan Davy (10)   65
Lydia Ross (9)   65
Joel Vickers (10)   66
Mark Dickinson (11)   66
Laura Stephenson (11)   67
Jaymie Welsh-Richardson (11)   67
Becki Stubbs (9)   68
Conor Hoop (10)   68
Natalie Wiles (10)   69
Jess Piercy (10)   69

Katy Gibbon (10)   70
Rachel Horsman (10)   70
Shauna Abbott (10)   71
Sarah Latteman (11)   72

Long Preston Primary School
Laura Hodgkiss (10)   72
Oliver Robinson (9)   73
Daniel F Thompson (7)   73
Eleanor Coultherd (9)   74
Alexander Cardwell (10)   74
Joseph Clark (7)   74
Stephanie Thompson (10)   75
Nancy Marchesi (10)   75
Michael Moon (8)   76

Mill Hill CP School
Kimberly Jayne Alderson (10)   76
Samantha Ross (9)   77
Natalie Gardiner (11)   77
Christina Stephenson (10)   78

Newby & Scalby Primary School
Molly Parker & Levon Barkhordarian (10)   78
George Allen (7)   78
Andrew Bryant & Sophie Smith (10)   79
Leah Sue-Ann Harrison (8)   79
Stacy Ness (7)   79
Alex Lenton (9)   80
Emma Botham (8)   80
Jacquetta Johnson (8)   80
Gabrielle J Flockton (7)   81
Jamie Muirhead (8)   81
Michael Tindall (7)   81
Nathan Corden (8)   82
Nicole Chapman (8)   82
Alexander Kirk (8)   82
Ione Wells (8)   83
Emily James (8)   83
Maddy Wood (7)   83

Euan David Riby (7)	84
Chrisopher Holmes (7)	84
Adele Swift (7)	84
Andrew Howson (9)	85
Matthew Richings (7)	85
Chloe Merritt (7)	86
Abhishek NG (7)	86
Amber-Rose McCrory (7)	86
Thomas Heaton (7)	87
Thomas Broughton (7)	87
Steven Broadbent (7)	87
Megan Woodward-Hay (7)	88
Georgiana Swalwell Pashby (7)	88
Sophie Williams (8)	88
Jessica Donnelly (9)	89
Harmony Hudgell (8)	89
Nick Perry (8)	89
Tzarini Meyler (8)	90
Adam Newbould (8)	90
David Shaw (8)	90
Daniel Petty (9)	91
Katie Hastie (8)	91
Katy Millions (9)	92
Connor Greenhough (8)	92
Anannyua Kumarvel (8)	92
Ben Allison (8)	93
Nell Baker (8)	93
Laura Davidson (8)	93
Samantha Greenham (8)	94
Jordan Kelly (8)	94
Sam Ellwood (9)	95
Hollie Rowe (9)	95
Eilish McCausland (11)	96
Daniel Riley (8)	96
Connor Ramsden (8)	97
Ellie Hornsby (10)	97
Frederick Jackson (10)	98
Mark Thompson (8)	98
Lucy Tindall (10)	99
Luke Botham (10)	99
Sophie Ness (11)	100
Alex Walker (10)	100

Andrew Trigg (9)   100
Emily Doveton (11)   101
Tom Newlove   101
Robert Wilson (11)   101
Niall Gibb (10)   102
Hanna Larrson (10)   102
Mollie Graham (10)   102
Amy Watkin (9)   103
Stephen Gaines (10)   103
Mark Jackson (10)   103
Tiffany Rowe (9)   104
Matthew Gibson (9)   104
Alistair Haythorne (9)   105
Adam Umpleby (9)   105
Matthew Machin (10)   106
Taylor Vasey (9)   106
Mathew Hume (10)   107
Sam Simmons (9)   107
Luke Corden (10)   107
Ben Allen (10)   108

Park Grove Primary School
Dominique Evans (10)   108
Rachel Hampton (10)   109
Imogen Cole (10)   109
Dipto Chowdhury (9)   110
Bethan Davies (9)   111
Jessica Dawson (9)   111
Louis Dickinson (10)   111
Isobel Gordon (9)   112

Riccall Primary School
Jack Coverdale, Scott Bellamy & Chris Brelsford (11)   112
Melissa Davies (8)   113
Nadine Moore (8)   113
Hannah Mizen (7)   114
Amy Dicks (7)   114
Isabelle LeMonnier (7)   115
Charlotte Horner (8)   115
Dean Frankish (11)   116
Andrew Beck & Karen Garbett (11)   116

St Mary's CE Primary School, York

Spennithorne CE Primary School

Ashleigh Arnold (7)	136
Daisy Roe (7)	136
Jeremy J Foster (7)	136
Ellie Cooke (8)	137
Will Stephenson (7)	137
Lloyd Plews (6)	137
Sophie Walton (7)	138
Emily Milverton (7)	138
Kate Kitchingman (7)	139
Callum Carlisle (7)	139
Amy Leathley (7)	140
Georgina Laws (7)	140
Emily Jefferson (7)	141

Stockton-on-the-Forest CP School

Jennifer Anderson (9)	141
Luke Howden (8)	142
Maya Blakeway (8)	142
Liam Coughlin (8)	143
Samantha Fraser (9)	143
Daniel Langford (7)	144
Jamie Richardson (8)	144
Danielle Bell (9)	145
Jordan Fletcher (7)	145
Tommy Hields (7)	146
Cassie Hields (8)	146
Abbie Seavers (8)	147
Bethany Raine (8)	147
Nathan Bargate (8)	147
Katherine Wilson (8)	148
Charlie Kirkpatrick (7)	148
Hannah Hall (8)	148
Jade Temperton (8)	149
Emma Hamilton (9)	149
Emma Whitson (8)	150

Thornton-in-Craven Community Primary School

Emma Leeming (8)	150
Alex Pilling (8)	150
Callum Higgins (8)	151

Emily Teall (7)   151
Alex Walker (7)   151
Alex Sharrad (9)   152
Milly Gates (9)   152
Dale Terry (9)   153
James Nicholas (8)   153
Sidney Shorten (8)   154
Stanley Bowley (9)   154
Sam Mavor (7)   154
Michael Stoker (8)   155

Thorpe Willoughby CP School
Jared Longhorne (11)   155
Eleanor Craven (11)   156
James Thomas (8)   157
Leah Mathias (9)   157
Emma Jennison (8)   157
Ailsa Stainthorpe (10)   158
Emma Gough (8)   158
Rebecca Coupland (10)   159
Sophie Billingsley (8)   159
Melissa Nix (9)   160
Emily Jackson (8)   161
Robert Chadwick (8)   162
Marcus Loveday (9)   162
Charlotte Karpow (11)   163
Sean Greenwood (10)   163
Sara Thompson (9)   164
Aimée Schofield (10)   164
Lora Barratt   165
Steven Flanagan (10)   165
Laura Hill (9)   166
Tom Wales (9)   166
Nadia Smith (10)   167
Stacey Nix (11)   168
Aimee Barratt (11)   169
Aaron Williams (10)   170
Victoria Amos (9)   170
Bethany Wadlow (9)   171
Sian McEvoy (8)   172
Craig May (8)   172

Lauren Golton (9)	173
Rebecca Cram (9)	173
Alex Parkin (9)	174
Joshua Humphrey-Shepherd (9)	174
Nicholas Bingham (9)	175
Stephanie Freer (8)	175
Maggie Hymes (9)	176
Matthew Wain (9)	177
Emily Burton (9)	178

West Heslerton CE Primary School

Jono Trowsdale (9) & William Ashton (10)	178
Matthew Marucci (9) & Daniel Burns (11)	179
Hannah Clay (11) & Louise Milner	179
Jenny Hyde (9) Sara Parker (9)	180
Thomas Parsons (10) & Jake Handley	180
Josephine Watson (10) & Leanne Pickering (10)	181
Charlie Ward (11)	181

The Poems

My Window

When I looked
Out of my
Window
I saw a star,
It was a special star
A star from afar.

When I looked
Out of my
Window
I saw the sun,
It reminded me of
Flowers,
And of having fun.

Abigail Long (9)
Ainderby Steeple CE Primary School

Peacock

Can you guess
That a slow and gentle peacock
Is the *king*?
Couldn't you see his fine
Cloak of sleek, royal
Feathers,
Or his indigo crown?
Did you?
Even if you couldn't see him
He can always see you
From behind
With his many
Turquoise
Eyes.

Erin Gill (8)
Ainderby Steeple CE Primary School

The Bear Who Was Mad About Hair

Once upon a time,
I wrote a little rhyme,
So here it is,
It's quite a whizz,
I hope you do not mind.

It's all about a bear,
Who didn't like his hair,
He gelled it loads,
And shaped some toads,
But still he didn't like it.

He then went to the barber's,
And ate fifteen bananas,
His hair was cut,
Till bald as a nut,
He *really* didn't like it.

So finally he left it,
And for all his life he kept it,
But then one day,
He had to say,
'I wish I'd never wrecked it!'

So he thought for another hobby,
And found a little jobby,
He worked for the bank,
And found a friend, Frank . ..
And it started all over again!

Timothy Foxford (8)
Ainderby Steeple CE Primary School

Hamsters

Hamsters look so cute and cuddly curled up in a ball,
They sleep all day, you wouldn't know they were there at all.
In the night they wake up and run, chew and play,
They are so tired the next day.

Catherine Pridmore (8)
Ainderby Steeple CE Primary School

School

When I went to school,
I trod in a pool.
I'll never forget,
Cos my feet were wet.

When I went to play,
Someone pushed in my way.
I fell on the floor,
And hurt my jaw.

When it was time for lunch,
My apple went *crunch!*
It flew in the air,
And I fell off my chair.

When I went home,
I had a good moan,
And then I felt calm,
Cos I'd come to no harm!

Saskia Fullerton-Smith (8)
Ainderby Steeple CE Primary School

Legs

Fat legs
Thin legs
Spotty legs
Wrinkly legs
Running legs
Slow legs
Fast legs
Scratchy legs
Chubby legs
I love legs.

George Easton (7)
Ainderby Steeple CE Primary School

Owl

If the day is night
Silence is drawn
People are asleep
Night animals are awake
Sound of snoring in the distance
Soft feathers all around his body
Hard legs at the bottom of his body
Night will never die!

Annabel Charlton (7)
Ainderby Steeple CE Primary School

There Was A Young Girl Called Lotty

There was a young girl called Lotty
Whose dog looked very dotty
He chewed a phone
Which he thought was a bone
So Lotty thought he was potty.

Bobbie Coleman (7)
Ainderby Steeple CE Primary School

The Dolphin

Dolphins dip like the waves
Fast and slow, dancing through the waves
They sing and call like birds
Shimmering like a golden sunbeam
Playing all day.

Megan Readman (8)
Ainderby Steeple CE Primary School

Schooltime

In my school I work and play,
Different things from day to day,
My teachers are so kind and true,
A happy day for me and you.

Every day we work so hard,
Writing, spellings, be on your guard,
The teachers will be after you,
There is no hiding, looby loo!

From 9 to 3 we work away,
But at lunchtime we have a play,
We eat our food and drink our drink,
Then it's back to work: you have to think.

Lucy Clarkson (9)
Ainderby Steeple CE Primary School

Scissors

Snip! Snip! Snippety snap,
That's all I do.
I slide and I glide,
Snippety snap.
I snap and snip again and again,
But that's all I do.
I love to snip and snap.
I do it every day.
The only time I don't snip is at zzzzz!

Emily Miller (8)
Ainderby Steeple CE Primary School

Dogs

I love dogs,
Big dogs,
Small dogs,
And in-between ones
I love puppies,
All round and cute even when they chew my boot.
They run and roll and love to play,
Even when it is the end of the day.

Sophie Glover (8)
Ainderby Steeple CE Primary School

Happiness

Happiness is yellow
It tastes like home-made chips
It smells like chocolate
It looks like fresh flowers
It sounds like birds chirping in the trees
It feels like I'm on cloud nine.

Claire Herrington (11)
Applegarth Primary School

Fear

Fear is red
and it tastes like sour lemons,
it smells like raw meat.
Fear looks like a deserted, blacked-out
underground station,
it sounds like dark, echoing footsteps,
it feels like some spiders are crawling on you.

Tom Weighell (11)
Applegarth Primary School

Happiness

Happiness is green
It tastes like chocolate cake
It smells like freshly-cut grass
It looks like a colourful town filled with people having fun
It sounds like beautiful music and laughing voices
It feels like you're on top of the world.

Harry Munton (10)
Applegarth Primary School

Excitement

Excitement is blue,
It tastes like chocolate,
It smells like fresh strawberries,
It looks like misty roads,
It sounds like the rustle of autumn leaves,
It feels like a gust of wind.

Gemma Anderton (10)
Applegarth Primary School

Anger

Anger is red
It tastes like super hot peppers
Anger smells like a forest fire
It looks like a jack hammer smashing concrete
Anger sounds like an earthquake's slow rumble
It feels like frustration!

Daniel Millward (10)
Applegarth Primary School

Happiness

Happiness is yellow,
It tastes like freshly picked strawberries,
Happiness smells like rose-scented candles,
It looks like my mum,
Happiness sounds like flowers swaying gently in the breeze,
It feels like home-made chocolate mousse.

Emily Richardson (11)
Applegarth Primary School

Happiness

It is the colour gold
It tastes of pears
It smells of my baby sister
It looks like Heaven
It sounds like my favourite band
Happiness feels all soft.

Curtis Carlton (10)
Applegarth Primary School

Happiness

The yellow comes out of my face
the taste is like chocolate
and it smells like fragrant flowers
it's like a pretty puppy
happiness is the best!

Alexandra Jefferson (10)
Applegarth Primary School

Loneliness

Loneliness is the colour grey,
It tastes like dry toast,
It smells like stagnant water,
Loneliness looks like a misty path,
It sounds like the wind rustling by,
It feels like being lost.

Jacques Peacock (11)
Applegarth Primary School

Happiness

Happiness is yellow,
It tastes like nice warm chocolate cake,
It smells like freshly-cut grass,
It looks like a street full of happy people,
It sounds like happy, friendly voices,
It feels like a room full of smiling faces.

Thomas Pattison (10)
Applegarth Primary School

Anger

Anger is red,
It tastes like spicy chillies,
And smells like petrol,
Anger looks like the burning sun,
It sounds like thunder echoing through a mountain range,
Anger feels like boiling water.

Jennie Thompson (10)
Applegarth Primary School

Happiness

Happiness is orange
It tastes like fresh fish and chips
And smells like petrol
Happiness looks like a golden gate in glistening sun
Happiness is laughter
Happiness is being over the moon.

Mitchell Marston (10)
Applegarth Primary School

Excitement

Colour is blue
It tastes like fresh toffee
And smells like fresh strawberries
It looks like a smiling sun
And sounds like the birds singing tunefully
It feels like you're a millionaire.

Nicola Clark (11)
Applegarth Primary School

The Creaky Tree

On Monday morning I went to see
Our new creaky chestnut tree
I was not sure on this tree
After all it was bigger than me!

On Monday night I couldn't sleep
For the creak of the tree was scaring me
I peaked out of my window
It started to stop
It could have been a he
For he was annoying me.

Katherine Head (9)
Bainbridge CE Primary School

A Football's Pain

Oh how I hate to be kicked,
Popped, burst and thrown about.
I like it when the goalkeeper catches me
In his nice, soft gloves.
I hate it when I am kicked up high,
Just to come down and land and bounce,
Or land on the roof of the stands.
Ouch!

Believe me, you don't want to be me.
I don't get kicked around anymore,
Thank You, Lord,
Because I got ripped while playing a game.
Hallelujah!

Joshua Prudden (9)
Bainbridge CE Primary School

The Bossy Teacher

Our teacher is a pain
He is always late for class
His name is Mr Main
He is always breaking glass

Some days he shouts
Other days he's quite kind
I think he is going
Out of his mind

He is rather nice
When he is in a good mood
But he can get bossy
When the boys are so rude.

Tamsin Alexander (10)
Bainbridge CE Primary School

Under The Sea

I fell off a boat
Into the dark sea
Creatures surrounding me

Apart from something spotted
Under a shell
Smiling at me.

A lighthouse light
Spinning round
Shining on me.

I swam deeper and deeper
Until . . . *something* . . .
Started chasing me.

I saw something behind me
A big, black shadow
Find out in the next poem of
Under the sea.

Katie-Jean Lambert (9)
Bainbridge CE Primary School

If I Was . . .

If I was a jumping frog
I would hop here and hop there.

If I was a smelly skunk
I would not go near you.

If I was a purring cat
I would not be lazy.

If I was a barking dog
I would be your best friend.

If I was someone else
I would not want to be
I just want to be me!

Becky Williams (7)
Bainbridge CE Primary School

Farm Poem

The cow is excited
But the sheep goes baa
They're so good together
They try to drive a car

A chicken goes cluck, cluck
And a dog goes woof
You know he's quite playful
Although he likes a huff

The farmer has a wife
He says she's very nice
The farmer says she makes lovely food
But the best is the rice

The pig and the sheep are good for one thing
They're lovely for your dinner
But they always make you fat
You would wish you could be thinner.

Isobel Bushby (9)
Bainbridge CE Primary School

Fishy Business

It's boring in my tank.
The water is so mucky.
I barely get fed.
They always forget me.
Once they tried teaching me tricks,
It didn't work.
I just forgot it instantly.
The only thing I remember
Is opening and shutting my mouth.
I really want to explore the ocean.
I'm a fish, get me out of here,
To the river,
Now.

Katie Seal (11)
Bainbridge CE Primary School

Being A Wrestling Ring Hurts!

Pain is all I feel
Pain, pain, pain, pain, pain
I've been bonked and bashed with all sorts
Steel chairs, tables, sledgehammers, ladders
I could go on forever.
You would hate being me.

Daniel Williams (9)
Bainbridge CE Primary School

The Gloomy Cave

One lovely sunny day
I took my dog out for a walk.
Jack, my dog, ran up to the top of the mountain.
From a distance all they could see was a lillle black hole.
What is it?

It was a cave.

Ross Thwaites (7)
Bainbridge CE Primary School

Snowmen Standing Cinquain

Snowmen,
Carrot noses,
Standing in the snowstorm,
Watery sunshine melting snow,
Snowmen.

Libby Lang-Burns (7)
Baldersby St James CE Primary School

Winter Fires Cinquain

Fires
Flames crackling
Orange warm lights glowing
Wet clothes drying round the fire
Fires.

Gilly Thorne (8)
Baldersby St James CE Primary School

Draughty Day Cinquain

Winter
Cold and draughty
Snow blowing through the door
I keep warm in front of fire
Chilly.

Jade Dunn (8)
Baldersby St James CE Primary School

Hedgehogs Cinquain

Winter,
Hedgehogs curl up,
Keeping warm under leaves,
Watching for the warm spring to come,
Sleeping.

Ben Hunt (9)
Baldersby St James CE Primary School

Icicles Cinquain

Winter,
Cold and freezing,
Jack Frost biting your toes,
Icicles hanging and dripping,
Shiver.

Megan Kettlewell (9)
Baldersby St James CE Primary School

Hedgehogs In The Winter Cinquain

Hedgehogs,
Hibernating,
Curled up warm in the leaves,
Dreaming of playing with their friends,
Winter.

Katie Utley (8)
Baldersby St James CE Primary School

Football Is The Best Sport

Football is the best sport,
Referees as strict as ice,
Policemen on guard for crowd trouble.
Linesmen darting around the edge of the pitch.
Footballers as nervous as deer.
But when they finally win
They're as happy as can be.

Alexandra Groom (9)
Birstwith CE Primary School

Hippo

Marble eyes sunk in his head,
Wallowing peacefully in the murky depths.

Big and wide enormous rump,
They all look ever so round and plump.

Thick and dry ashen skin,
Always wears a great big grin.

Under the mud for special cover,
Youngsters rest beside their mothers.

Gazing across the vast plain,
Looking at the swooping and diving crane.

Gaping nose holes side by side,
Flattish muzzle, mud has been applied.

Little tail waving madly,
Scaring flies but doing badly.

They look so sweet and cuddly,
Until they decide to *charge* at *me!*

Jessica Umpleby (10)
Birstwith CE Primary School

The Hunt

The eagle in his tree
Looks around up high then down below,
He looks to the right and then the left.
He spots a rabbit far below,
He takes off as quiet as a mouse,
He soars through the branches as fast as a cheetah
To catch up with his prey.
He dives and now he is just centimetres away.
He tries to bite,
He misses.
But then the rabbit disappears down a hole.
So I'm afraid the eagle will stay hungry for a while longer.

Jacob Eastland (10)
Birstwith CE Primary School

Robot

One ton of heavy metal, not quite as dainty as a petal,
radiation smells and wires so fine, wires like ivy, wires like vine.
Plods along like a heavy tortoise, squeaks and rattles, quite a noise.
A screen instead of an eye that can see X-ray sights,
a screen that flickers and flashes like lights.
Its gentle clamps can be used for washing up,
can do even harder jobs like brushing the pup.
Sometimes he gets a low battery and has to charge it,
you can tell when he is charging because a dull light is lit.
It stands for fourteen hours or more, makes a quiet mumble snore.
Then he wakes up with a bound and a full battery,
he walks into the kitchen making noises quiet and pattery.
Its metal head moves around on its smooth metal neck,
he sees blazing in sunlight, he watches the birds peck.
A robot does break at the first sign of water
the robot is breaking, here comes Mum and daughter.
Brother, Father, everyone,
the robot's broken, now the robot's work is done.

Kaya Oldaker (10)
Birstwith CE Primary School

Waterfall

Splashing down its slippery rocks
Covered in moss and leaves,
Comes water tossing and turning,
Skidding down, down, down, down . . .

Until *'splosh'*
The water tumbles down
And searches the area into all the thin gaps
Until again falling, falling, falling, falling . . .

And the fast flowing, clear, clean water
'Bounces' to the bottom until again flowing,
Flowing, flowing, flowing . . .

Kate Rollerson (9)
Birstwith CE Primary School

The Pensieve

Creeping up the dark red steps,
The door as blue as sea.
The creaking door slowly opening,
Walking in as quiet as a mouse.
Looks left and right and up the stairs,
Opens a second mystical door.
Then he saw as white as snow,
Swirly mist in a basin of black.
Takes his wand and slowly pokes,
Head first he falls in.
Like a dolphin diving in,
Into a dark, dank room.
Parting people, darting all over,
Looking for a door and a way out.
Then there come creatures two,
Scaly hand reaching out.
Breath as sharp as a sharp, sharp knife,
Then falling down, falling, falling . . .

Adam Willford (11)
Birstwith CE Primary School

Fantasy In A Forest

There's a dragon in the forest,
Its purple wings leathery and tough,
And the tail scented with a poisonous touch.
As fast as lightning,
As swift as wind,
This powerful creature spies the land like a bird of prey.
Higher and higher,
Faster and faster,
Going from sight,
And going further.
Going,
Going,
Gone!

Helen Hovell (10)
Birstwith CE Primary School

A Mouse Called . . . ?

I'm white, brown, small and slim,
speedy, plus I'm scared to death, I'm just
so cute and cuddly you just can't resist me.

I'm ticklish, tiny, quick and cute,
it's time for playtime, out you go,
I'm quick as lightning, soft as silk,
I'm so annoying, I soon get on your nerves.

I'm just so messy not like you lot,
you are clean, well at least I think so,
I am always trying to get out of the cage,
I am also sneaky, cuddly and have black eyes.
I'm naughty 'cause I chew all of the toilet roll to pieces.
I have cute and tiny ears.

I'm giddy, jumpy, noisy and sweet,
I have a long tail. Just before you get to sleep,
I always try to keep you awake,
when I get out of the cage I try to escape.

By the way, my name is Fudge!

Hayley Metcalfe (10)
Birstwith CE Primary School

A Dolphin

Gliding like a ghost,
Cutting through the water as quick as lightning,
Feeling like a wet welly,
Grey, as it slips silently through the waves,
Diving down like an Olympic diver,
The friendly click, like a wheel going round,
The acrobat of the sea!

The beautiful body slipping over the water,
A sudden splash does not move the dolphin,
It bravely battles on through the chop of the waves,
Quickly it spots a boat and glides over,
Jumping up in the wake of the boat,
The tourists come and take photos,
The acrobat of the sea.

His small white belly and his little bottlenose head,
All bobbing in the water like a used cork,
The seagulls dive and splash in the waves,
Also the puffins come out for a meal,
Suddenly a dorsal fin emerges from the water . . .
But luckily it is only another dolphin come to play,
The acrobats of the sea.

Kate Robinson (10)
Birstwith CE Primary School

The Horse

As quick as lightning,
The horse galloping,
Looking around like an eagle looking for its prey,
Dancing on the moors,
Going over rivers, over fields,
Gliding over walls like a bird gliding in the sky.

The horse, moving around like a black shadow at night,
The horse lives on moors,
Roaming around like a lion on the plains.
It drinks from the streams,
That flow like a person running.
It has no friend to be in his herd.

As quick as lightning,
The horse galloping,
Dancing on the moors,
And going over rivers, over fields,
A loud *bang!* startles the horse,
Off it hurtles away, galloping, galloping . . .

Emma Waddington (10)
Birstwith CE Primary School

The Life Of A Waterfall

The waterfall, tall and long
Stands still every day,
As the water falls from the top
And rushes down to the bottom,
Down and down it goes.

The waterfall sounds like
A television out of tune,
It comes down faster than sound,
As it hits the sharp rocks,
As it makes them wet and slimy.

So as the water goes down from it,
It stays standing still every night and day.

Mark Foster (11)
Birstwith CE Primary School

The Dolphin

A splash of water sprayed like water from a hose,
A tail fin, then a head and a bottlenose.
Clicking to communicate to other friends,
Enjoying all the precious time together that they spend.

A grey head, a little white belly,
These are the tricks we see on the telly!
Bobbing up and down through the waters down beneath,
Doing fantastic tricks, showing off underneath.

A splash of water sprayed like water from a hose,
A tail fin, then a head and a bottlenose.
Clicking to communicate to other friends,
Enjoying all the precious time together that they spend.

Swimming with humans, helping at need,
Dodging round little clumps of seaweed.
Escorting the boats round the bumpy bends,
Helping with errands, the messages send!

A splash of water sprayed like water from a hose,
A tail fin, then a head and a bottlenose.
Clicking to communicate to other friends,
Enjoying all the precious time together that they spend!

The dolphin jumps, goes through the loop,
Look, the next one she does is the hoop.
She flies like an acrobat but there's the ding,
Now she has been called to go out of the ring.

A splash of water sprayed like water from a hose,
A tail fin, a head and a bottlenose.
Clicking to communicate to other friends,
Enjoying all the precious time together that they spend.

Cleone Pardoe (10)
Birstwith CE Primary School

The Kitten

Sitting by the fire purring gently,
Sea of happy faces stroking the dear,
Sweet kitten, you have nothing to fear, its fur golden as the sun.

The kitten pouncing wall to wall, garden to garden,
Searching for new adventures.

Its cute purr gaining attention,
The gentle paw is in the air,
Soft eyes looking at your hair,
The cuddly kitten loves you.

The kitten pouncing wall to wall, garden to garden,
Searching for new adventures.

In the nightfall the kitten goes out into the dark never afraid,
Of the owl hooting at its very best,
The rattling of the trees,
Where the kitten never rests,
The streets lamps on, making scary shadows of everything around.

The kitten pouncing wall to wall, garden to garden,
Searching for new adventures.

The sleepy kitten comes in,
Yawning as the sun rises.
Its body drooping to bed, to sleep it must
To sleep until dusk,
The sky is pink and orange, it is dawn,
The kitten sleeps.

The kitten pouncing wall to wall, garden to garden,
Searching for new adventures.

Josie Caven (10)
Birstwith CE Primary School

The Marathon

The start of the marathon,
I'm standing there waiting for the buzzer to go off.

Beep!

And off I go, the leader of the group,
Pacing myself to go as quick as lightning at the end.

I think to myself, *keep going keep the pace going,*
Head to the left, keep the pace going,
In through the nose,
Out through the mouth,
Keep the pace going.

Gasping for a drink,
I can see the water station
Oh that's better!

I think to myself, *Keep the pace going,*
Head to the left, keep the pace going,
In through the nose,
Out through the mouth,
Keep the pace going.

Up the road round the corner
Look over my shoulder to see who's there
I can see the finish line,
I am the one the only one,
So I run as quickly as lightning,

I've gone through the line,
Yes!
I've won!

Megan Caven (10)
Birstwith CE Primary School

The Tiger

In the dark, gloomy forest a tiger is moving silently
Creeping through the forest green
Waiting for its prey.
Ready to pounce.
Waiting, waiting, waiting.
The antelope *'crashes'* down to the ground
And the tiger crunches chewy meat off the antelope
Now the tiger is full
It slowly walks away
Leaving the remains of the poor antelope
Now the tiger slowly walks back to his territory
And the tiger falls asleep
After the tiger goes for another . . .
     Kill!
Following on the tiger goes for a cool, refreshing drink
At the waterhole
The tiger slowly laps the water
In the spiky hot sun
He walks into cool water
And goes for a swim
Then all of a sudden he spots something
     A zebra
And *darts* out of the water and
Peruses it, the tiger misses it and slowly plods home
Back to his
     Den!

Sophie Hodgson (11)
Birstwith CE Primary School

Waterfall

Calmly the water flows
Moving quietly,
Between the hard, cold rocks,
Slowly getting fast and faster
Then it stops,
Then like a roller coaster
It tumbles down and down
Then crash!
The water hits the bottom
Fast as lightning.

Quickly the water trickles
Pushing small rocks aside,
At the bottom of the stream
Light, puffy, bubbly foam waits
Till the water takes it away.

Ehlana Hodgson (11)
Birstwith CE Primary School

The Old House

Tick-tock goes the grandfather clock
like a tiger waiting in suspense for its prey,
Then the bed in the corner all worn yet still comfy,
The carpet on the floor all grey and gloomy,
The armchair in the middle once lilac but now grey,
The television all fuzzy and wonky
with the aerial all bent and hanging down,

The kitchen is in a right mess,
There are pots and pans everywhere
Hardly any food in the fridge,
There's the oven in the corner all brown,
crispy and greasy,
The dishcloths are streaky and dirty,
The windows are as black as night.

Emma Groom (9)
Birstwith CE Primary School

Why?

Why is the sky blue?
Why is the grass green?
Why are houses made of bricks and not margarine?

Why are there trees in a forest?
Why are there stars in the sky?
Why can't birds have feet and humans be allowed to fly?

Why are there ladies and men?
Why are there girls and boys?
Why can't we have as much money as we want and buy
all our favourite toys?

Why do we live on Earth?
Why can't we live on the moon?
Why can't we live forever instead of dying so soon?

Emily Reynard (10)
Birstwith CE Primary School

Arron's Dream

What will I be when I grow up,
I haven't got a clue,
I really have no idea what I'm going to do.

Maybe a soldier in the army I'll be,
With guns, tanks and dirt,
I'd shout a lot with a camouflaged face,
Maybe not! I might get hurt.

Maybe an airline pilot I'd be,
Flying around the sky,
I'd take my mum to Italy,
For some pizza pie.

Maybe a footballer I'd be,
With goals, penalties and cool hair,
I could marry someone like Posh Spice,
Wouldn't we make a good pair!

Arron Gent (9)
Carnagill County Primary School

Wintertime Is White

W intertime is bold,
 I nside children are cold,
N uts and berries are off the trees,
T he mice are eating all the cheese,
E nter the cold and the frost,
R unning to the snowman but it is lost.
T rees are blowing in the breeze,
 I n my trousers trembling knees,
M e and friends in the snow,
E veryone is on the go.

 I s Santa on his way?
S nowbells ringing on the sleigh.

W ith presents for you and me,
H as he got the spare key?
 I sit in my bed and rest my head,
T hen it is morning instead,
E xcited because it is *Christmas!*

Jasmine Lindsey (10)
Carnagill County Primary School

The Lost Head

There was a young man
Who couldn't decide
Whether he wanted
To laugh or cry,
He was sitting on the fence
Deciding what to do,
He was feeling hot under the collar,
He got in a bit of bother,
And took a tumble
Then lost his head too.

Daniel Kenny (11)
Dishforth Airfield Community Primary School

My Mates In My Class

A   is for Austin who likes to play
B   is for Ben who is messy with clay
C   is for Cathy who loves choir
D   is for Daniel who is a liar
E   is for Eleanor who is very sweet
F   is for Fred who would do anything but cheat
G   is for Georgina who bets
H   is for Heather who has 15 pets
I   is for Ian who has a girlfriend
J   is for Jenny who would lend
K   is for Kellie who has neat writing
L   is for Lydia who does not like fighting
M   is for Matthew who's best at maths
N   is for Nathan who never baths
O   is for Owen who has spiky hair
P   is for Paul who would not share
Q   is for Quentin who has a suntan
R   is for Reece who's mad about Jackie Chan
S   is for Steven who likes apple pie
T   is for Thomas who would never lie
U   is for Ursula who wears no shoes
V   is for Vicky who hangs around in the loos
W   is for William who is always sad
X   is for Xenia who fancies the lads
Y   is for Yasmin who has smelly feet
Z   is for Zoe who wears a white sheet.

Alexandra Quinn (10)
Dishforth Airfield Community Primary School

This Little Lion

This little ding dong lion had a very small life
And his inny winny roar sounded like his wife
Ping! Came a fairy in a dingly dangly cape
And said, 'I can ping you into any shape.'
'Make me gigantic and not small
And louden my inny winny call.'
With a ping ding fing ding
He turned into a king.

Steven Stewart (10)
Dishforth Airfield Community Primary School

When I'm Dirty

When I'm dirty I'm not that clean,
My mum says I look incredibly mean.
I don't really care at all,
Until she says,
'Let's go and get you new clothes at the mall.'
Or even worse, 'Go have a bath.'

Jennifer McMillan (11)
Dishforth Airfield Community Primary School

Winter

In winter when the fields are white,
the sun doesn't shine so bright.
Little people have snowball fights
you'd better stay out of it . . .
If you go in one, some snowballs are
made of ice and may hurt you
The snowmen might fall on you
and you will be lost . . .

Jamie Noble (9)
Foston CE Primary School

My Guinea Pig Buttercup

My guinea pig . . .
Is a cuddly, fluffy, smooth thing.
Her fur is soft, ginger and black
She just sits on your knee and lays there.

My guinea pig . . .
Is called Buttercup.
Her favourite food is celery,
She's the most active of the two.

My guinea pig . . .
She is a cute thing
Her age is 3.
She is greedy, such a pig . . . but I love her.

Jessica Woardby (9)
Foston CE Primary School

Perfect Pets

Guinea pigs in a hutch,
Eating far too much.

When you stroke their silky fur,
You'll know that they're really there.

When you feed the guinea pigs,
They grow very, very big.

When you clean the hutch,
You'll notice it smells too much.

The best thing about guinea pigs,
Is that they look like they have wigs.

Lianne Noble (11)
Foston CE Primary School

Carlos The Mighty

Standing at the window,
A beautiful girl,
Round her neck,
Sparkling pearls,
A ring on her finger,
Engaged to a man,
Today they would meet by the barn.

Out from behind her there came a hand,
Covered her mouth,
Dragged her into the sand,
Then to the barn, she was stranded there,
With the vicious villain,
Ruben Falcane.

Out in the darkness,
Who should be there,
But Miranda's true love,
With his long pinned back hair,
His name was Carlos and he loved her so,
But when she never met him he thought he might go,
To where he was born 20 years ago.

He heard a cry,
Coming from the barn,
It was Miranda his true love,
He rescued her,
And sent Ruben to above.

Then they wed on a beautiful day,
When all spirits were high and gay,
So they lived together for evermore,
And they always remembered that special day,
When Carlos the mighty scared Ruben away.

Megan Bell (11)
Hambleton CE Primary School

The Floating Fluter

In the manor,
On top of the hill,
Where the bats fly low,
Where spooky things are on show,
Lives a flute player,
But she isn't ordinary.
She plans deadly things,
In her dark, dark lair.

There was a party at the manor,
One dark, starry night,
And among the people in fancy dress,
Was a young pretty girl named Bess,
Who had heard that the mansion was haunted,
But she wanted to see for herself.

Down in the cellar, was an ear-piercing noise,
Bess who was very brave,
Walked down the stone steps,
And there she saw a big, black chest,
Out came the flute player,
Bess stepped back, then . . .
Searing pain,
Everything went black.

The flute player played a soft sweet tune,
For she knew that soon,
Bess would join her in her lair,
And they would kill whoever enters there,
So beware!

Anna Wynne (10)
Hambleton CE Primary School

Granny And The Big Bad Pig

Once upon a time and thus begins our little rhyme,
Katie went to see her granny one day,
Through the town on her way,
Stopping to buy some cake and sherry,
Which will make her granny merry.
When she stopped she met a pig,
With a long ginger wig.
Then she carried on her way.
What a gloriously beautiful day.
The pig followed on,
Then he was gone.
When she was there,
She sat on a pear.
She looked at the bed,
Granny sure looked like she was dead.
Then she knew it was the pig,
With the long ginger wig.
Then she knew her granny had gone,
When Katie had an idea to kill the evil pig.
She went to the fireplace
And picked up the poker
Then poked the evil pig in his black heart.
She ran into the kitchen
And picked up a knife
Then split open the pig and out popped Granny.
Then she decided to dig
A grave for the big bad pig.
In the end they settled down in front of the telly
Katie had coke and Granny had sherry.

Emily Barlow (10)
Hambleton CE Primary School

Seasons

Spring

S pring is here
P eople are loving the warmth
R abbits are being born
I ce and snow melts away
N ow it's spring
G o mad!

Summer

S ummer is here
U nder the shining sun
M any people are sunbathing
M usic, fun and laughter
E ating burgers from the barbecue
R elax now!

Autumn

A utumn is here
U mbrellas blowing inside out
T umbling leaves falling down
U ntil the trees are bare
M any people are celebrating the harvest
N ext - winter!

Winter

W inter is here
I cicles forming everywhere
N ewly fallen snow covers the ground
T he cold weather is really here
E xcited children wait for Christmas
R oll on spring!

Emma Pendlebury (9)
Hambleton CE Primary School

Aztec Sleeping Beauty

The Aztec palace loomed up above,
From a hatch in the roof came a royal dove,
Bearing a message from the king,
To the citizens with gifts to bring.

To the royals a princess was born,
Her eyes were the colour of a magnificent dawn,
Aurora's golden locks fell down to her chin,
When suddenly the Aztec gods rushed in.

The hummingbird beauty did give,
Parrot goddesses helped the forest to live,
All the gods had their turn,
But then the witch of the night stalked in, her name was Burn.

She cursed the baby on her 13th birthday with death,
Then turned, flew away on the wind's cold breath.
The god, the jaguar appeared and said,
'I cannot break the spell, but she shall sleep and not be dead.'

Aurora awoke on her 13th birthday,
And thought how the years had flown away.
But Aurora did not know the curse upon her,
When she put on her lovely lemur fur.

Aurora went to the attic to see her soon to be inherited city.
There in the room was a lady old and witty.
She offered the princess a go at her spindle,
Once the girl fell, Burn's ire did not dwindle.

Some years later, when the court was in mourning,
A prince rode to the door through the turquoise dawning.
The prince, called Karm,
Gave the princess a kiss, which roused her like a charm.

She awoke and he asked her to marry him now,
Soon they ruled over all, *wow!*

Laura Perry (9)
Hambleton CE Primary School

The Giant Dragonfly

The fastest dragonfly
Began to grow in a blink of an eye
It burnt a house down to ash
And made the pipes go clish clash
Here comes Dom the mighty
While a girl was still asleep in her nighty
He had some fireproof nets
In the pub people were still playing bets
He lured the dragonfly to the trap
And the nets fell on the dragonfly with a big slap
The dragonfly had a humungous head
When the dragonfly fell over it was dead
The town had been called Blaze
Then they named it Dom and Dom stood there
And they were amazed.

Mark Pooleman (10)
Hambleton CE Primary School

Snow

Who saw the footprints in the snow?
Who came along and where did she go?

The farmer's wife has just been out
To scatter bits of bread about.

Who saw the footprints in the snow?
Who came along and where did she go?

One little sparrow was out today
He ate some bread and hopped away.

Who saw the footprints in the snow?
Who came along and where did she go?

Thea Muscroft (10)
Hambleton CE Primary School

When It Gets Dark

It's all dark now
I'm sitting in my bed
All the shadows are
Dancing on the walls
I start to shiver
All a quiver.

It's still dark
Gargoyles and ghosts
Are making fun of me
I hide under the covers
And start to cry
Boo Hoo!

It's really dark now
I hear a noise
Boom Boom
The door opens and . . .
Mum walks in
I'm not scared of the dark
Are you?

Lauren Dunwell (9)
Hambleton CE Primary School

Bubblegum

My bubblegum, my bubblegum
It keeps taking me up to the sky
But I can't understand why
It's only a little bubble
And it keeps popping on the branches
It's very unpleasant you know
One day my mother banned it from me
And that was the end of it you see
And over the next years
There were many tears
About the bubblegum that my mother threw away.

Rachel Cullen (9)
Hambleton CE Primary School

My Dinosaur

I thought dinosaurs were extinct,
Until I found one in the kitchen sink.
I jumped back in extreme surprise,
When an egg hatched before my very eyes!

Mum came down the stairs and screamed,
The dinosaur had grown!
I don't know what came over me,
I closed my eyes.

When I opened them I saw
A mouth came closer
Bye-bye me
Bye-bye Mum
Bye-bye world.

Emily Davies (9)
Hambleton CE Primary School

I Prefer

I play out,
I prefer home.
I go to shops,
I prefer home.
I buy stuff,
I prefer home.
I go horse riding,
I prefer home.
I go to my grandma's house,
I prefer home.
I go to school,
I prefer home.
I get grounded,
I prefer playing out.

Joanna Hopkinson (10)
Hookstone Chase CP School

It's Not Fair

It's not fair I have to get up early
It's not fair my hair is so curly
It's not fair my sister is so girly
It's just not fair.

It's not fair my teacher is so grumpy
It's not fair my bed is so lumpy
It's not fair because I'm a little monkey
It's just not fair.

Sophie Sadler (9)
Hookstone Chase CP School

My Dog

My dog isn't one of the ordinary.
He is very special to me,
He'll stay in my heart forever,
But I sometimes wish he'd leave me be.

My dog loves a belly scratch,
Very, very often,
Normally he likes swimming,
But I sometimes wish *he'd leave me be!*

Amy Rose Humphrey (8)
Hookstone Chase CP School

My Home

Through the squeaking door
The creaking floorboard
You can hear the dripping tap
Shattering bulbs hanging below
Music booming all the time.

Adam Hodgson (11)
Hookstone Chase CP School

Parents

Parents are a rare species
And are very weird and strange.
But you have to admit
They're as soft as fleeces
And get paid a very high wage.
They always hog electrical appliances
And never ever listen
But they always give you hugs and kisses
And should never be put in prison
They think they're always always right
And seem to get their own way
They're quite an ugly sight
But they'll change one day.

Mia Kilpatrick (11)
Hookstone Chase CP School

Winter

Icy whispers echo from cold mouths
Winter is on its way
Winter has come and might never go
Bitterly cold hands will have winter tucked away
Gold sunlight will never return
We might have sold the dazzling sun
Some other countries might have won the sun
And lost the winter
Here's where we win the sun or spring but best of all
Winter's now gone.

Olivia Connolly (8)
Hookstone Chase CP School

The Wolf

One foggy dark cold night,
One scared girl walked in the church light.
Suddenly she heard a startling howl,
Some wolves appeared and started to growl,
The chase was on.
Up the church stairs they went one step by one,
The top came soon, trapped in a corner,
There's no escape at all for her,
She stepped up on the wall,
Standing so straight but small,
Two choices she had,
But both looked rather bad,
She chose to chase it and was left
Falling, falling, falling . . .

Martin Priestley (11)
Hookstone Chase CP School

My Mum's Driving Drives Me Mad

My mum's driving drives me mad
Even my dad says that it drives him mad.

My mum's driving drives me mad
I wish that I could be driving.

My mum's driving drives me mad
Especially when she drives over flower beds
And down one-way streets.

My mum's driving drives me mad
When she drives me round roundabouts six times.

That's my mum!

Chloë Ince-Knight (11)
Hookstone Chase CP School

My Home

In my house I can hear the clock ticking
In my house I can hear my cat licking
In my house it is nice and quiet
But then my family arrive
And my house becomes alive
People chattering
Pots clattering
The TV talking
The washer humming
But then later in bed
Hush!

Joanne Allcock (11)
Hookstone Chase CP School

Alien Parents

Last night I woke with a shock
I heard the clock go tick-tock, tick-tock.
I slid down the bannister,
Only to see something so sinister,
But my mum's eyes popping out of her head!
I stared for a moment, too scared to speak,
Then I came to my senses and went back to sleep.
I replayed it over and over again.
I was beginning to believe it was just a dream when . . .
A head popped round the door only to say,
'Come on, lazy bones, we're off to Mars today!'

Megan Davies (10)
Hookstone Chase CP School

Cat In The Window What Do You See?

Cat in the window what do you see?
A dog called Fred sitting near me
Orders being given by the teacher near me
They are super kids, well so they say.
You see the target board and they are close to bullseye
The light of the window coming through distracts
One of the pupils flicks the window and I run off.

Mathew Wills (10)
Hookstone Chase CP School

My House

My house buzzes around like a bee
The doorbell goes pop, bang, wee!
The bathroom splishes and sploshes around in the waves.
The cooker sizzles and slides across the kitchen floor.
The boom in the background is just the front room door.
The washing on the floorboards, not being whizzed away.
But in my bedroom there is a slosh, slash, drip.

Amie Tipling (11)
Hookstone Chase CP School

The Boy From York

There once was a boy from York
Who's brother was an orc
He wears lots of armour
And he has a pet llama
And he eats lots of pork.

Tom Flynn (11)
Hookstone Chase CP School

My Dog Jess

My dog Jess lies in her bed taking a nap!
My dog Jess just eats and eats.
My dog Jess is big and fat.
My dog Jess is warm and cuddly.
I love Jess she's the best!

Melanie Saville (11)
Hookstone Chase CP School

Sadie

S lept very quietly
A loud noise awakened her
D reamt of her meal times
I watched her chase the birds
E very day I know she is there for me.

Rebecca Leigh (11)
Hookstone Chase CP School

My Rabbit Snowdrop

Snowdrop is grey and white,
Also doesn't fight,
She always likes her sweetcorn,
And her green beans,
But the best of all she loves mum and me.

Katie Fenn (9)
Hookstone Chase CP School

Parents

Dad sits in front of the telly,
Patting his big beer belly.
Mum tidies the entire house,
Even Whitey, my pet mouse!
I'm never going to be as fussy as Mum,
She never chews gum!
'Too messy,' she says,
Just like my ways!
I'm never going to be as lazy as Dad,
If I wanted to be like him, I'd be mad!
I'm happy being who I am,
Don't want to be my parents, just myself Pam,
Pam,
Pam,
Just myself Pam.

Almasa Pašalic (10)
Hookstone Chase CP School

Loneliness Is . . .

Loneliness is solitary,
forlorn,
unhappy.
Loneliness is isolated,
uninhabited,
alone.
Loneliness is abandoned,
destitute,
lonely-hearted.
Loneliness is remote,
estranged,
apart.

Robert Ellis (11)
Hookstone Chase CP School

Weird Parents!

Parents are the funniest things,
They think they know what's best,
Constantly drinking coffee and tea,
I admit that they're the strangest!

Living in their grown-up world,
Embarrassing around my friends,
They're sloppy - kissing hug machines,
But their loving never ends!

They're aliens from outer space,
From a world of frying pans,
Cooking and cleaning all day long,
With six thousand hands!

Kirsty Hunter (11)
Hookstone Chase CP School

My Home-Made Monster

He cries and cries and cries all night,
His eyes are like big fried eggs,
He goes purple when he wants his food,
His fingers are like wooden pegs,
He has a totally awful dress sense,
But my mum picks them out for him,
He kicks and kicks and kicks me,
He makes such an awful din,
He makes a fuss over what he eats,
Unfortunately he's my baby brother!

Gabriella Cooper (10)
Hookstone Chase CP School

My Home

Ping went the microwave,
Smash went the plate,
Whirr went the VCR,
At a slowing rate.

Clatter went the saucepans,
Chink went the glass,
Rustle went the sweetwrapper,
The sweet was really class.

Brynmor Powell (10)
Hookstone Chase CP School

Football

Football is my favourite game
Scoring is the best
But saving shots is just as good.
Making passes soar through the air
Landing on the striker's head.
Tackling players is just like robbery,
But best of all is to play in the game
And that is the best goal of all!

Jonny Allan (10)
Hookstone Chase CP School

The Moon

Look at that big white ball,
Some people call it the moon,
Mummy says there's a man on there,
But I don't think that's true.
If it's true,
I'd like to know him,
And see what it's like to live up there.

Jodie McCarthy (10)
Hookstone Chase CP School

My Brother Josh

My brother Josh is the best brother in the world
Even though he's normally a pain,
He's really a softie and humble inside
And that's why he's the best brother in the world.

My brother Josh is a whizz at computers
My brother Josh loves sausages and cheese
My brother Josh loves to have a laugh
And that's why he's the best brother in the world.

My brother Josh has a great personality
My brother Josh has really curly hair
I couldn't wish for another brother,
And that's why he's the best brother in the world.

Bethany Balla (10)
Hookstone Chase CP School

The Dodo!

The dodo is extinct. The dodo has died,
The dodo has disappeared and it won't come alive.
The dodo lived by the coast when the tide came in,
No dodos near the water because of the hunter's sin.
The dodo was white, with an orange beak,
With soft feathers, soft and sleek.
How we miss the dodo badly,
As sad as we can see,
That we know that this is sadly,
The hunter's jealousy.

Caitlin Chang (10)
Hookstone Chase CP School

Confused

I asked my mum one night
If I could have a frostbite
She said ask your dad
So I went to my dad
And he said ask your mum
I tried to tell him that I asked mum
But he wouldn't listen!
So I asked mum and she said
the same thing again and again.

I just got so confused!

Romy Jade Anderson (10)
Hookstone Chase CP School

My Family

My mum is the best mum in the world
She is always there when I need her
My dad he is pretty much the same
Although he's always watching the football game.
My brother he's alright I suppose
But we are always fighting with each other
Hattie my dog she is a ball full of fluff
My dog Hattie can do all sorts of stuff
And me I'm just
Perfect!

Georgina Smith (10)
Hookstone Chase CP School

My Grandad

My grandad was a very kind man,
My grandad was the funniest man,
My grandad was the cuddliest man,
My grandad was a generous man,
My grandad was an intelligent man,
My grandad was the cleverest man,
By my grandad has passed away,
But most of all he is still here with me
And is the best grandad in the world to me.

Katie Head (9)
Hookstone Chase CP School

Being Blind

Think of a mum who's glad, glad, glad,
Think of a dad who's mad, mad, mad,
Think of a nurse without a smile,
Think of a doctor who lost your file,
But I'll always have my family wherever they are,
And they will always be in my heart.

Katy Walters (10)
Hookstone Chase CP School

Cheddar Cheese

Cheddar cheese is the best
It looks like the sun and tastes like cream
And all of the different flavours have their own taste
But all of them taste the same to me.

Oliver Chapman (9)
Hookstone Chase CP School

Football Mad

Chelsea, Chelsea aren't so good,
Chelsea, Chelsea always fall in mud,
Leeds, Leeds are so bad,
Leeds, Leeds are so sad,
Man U, Man U are at the top,
Man U, Man U like pop,
Arsenal, Arsenal are The Gunners,
Arsenal, Arsenal are like brothers,
Newcastle, Newcastle are The Magpies
Newcastle, Newcastle are the bad guys.

Elliott Gray (10)
Hookstone Chase CP School

Gathering Leaves

A utumn, golden crunchy leaves
U nder the trees they lay
T ouching the ground softly
U ntil it's time to go away.
M ice scuttling in the undergrowth
N oon sunlight, gleaming all day.

L eaf fights are so much fun,
E xciting playtimes in the leaves.
A fternoon tea under the trees
V eins standing out on the leaves,
E arthy damp smells fill the air
S treams flowing in the green.

Millie Sanderson (10)
Ingleby Arncliffe CE Primary School

Autumn Has Come

The dark autumn night
The squirrels flee with fright
Dark as it may be
You can still see the leaves on the trees.
The silver moon in the sky,
Birds no longer fly.
The jack-o'-lanterns laugh
The leaves cover the path,
Morning has come.
Sun rises on the juicy plum,
Sunburnt brown conkers,
Squirrels going bonkers!
Growing pumpkins, nice and fat,
Children get their coats and hats,
So they can enjoy the day.

Hannah Miles (10)
Ingleby Arncliffe CE Primary School

Blizzard

I can destroy houses and factories,
I can kill people who are unfortunate to be in the way,
I am a cold, lethal killer
I don't come often but when I do
I am feared
I am a big whirlwind of cold, white bullets
I am an evil murderer of houses
I am a nice guy in an angry body.
Who am I?

Ben Stephenson (11)
Ingleby Arncliffe CE Primary School

Winter

Snow and ice is great but doesn't last,
Yet, it's very nice but not when it comes
With a blast.

Winter is great, since Christmas is in it
With turkey as bait and roads covered in grit.

Winter brings ice, winter brings snow
And days are shorter and spirits are never low
And never let the warmness falter.

Sachin Kumarendran (9)
Ingleby Arncliffe CE Primary School

Autumn Is Here

Autumn is here and all the leaves
fall down on the pavement, under the trees.

The leaves, as crisp as frost,
fall down as their home in the tree, is now lost.

Listen! Silence! Not a sound -
as golden brown leaves fall down to the ground.

Emma Barlow (10)
Ingleby Arncliffe CE Primary School

Hailstone

I am hard and cold
I am round
I fall super fast from the sky
I normally come in the winter
As soon as I hit something, I melt
Whenever someone sees me they run inside
I hurt when I land on you.

David Carr (10)
Ingleby Arncliffe CE Primary School

Autumn

Autumn leaves
Corn in sheaves,
Leaves we're hauling
Nuts are falling.

Birds and squirrels storing,
Autumn animals, yawning,
Leaves twirling
Winds whirling.

Autumn leaves everywhere,
Blackberries over there.
Bushes and trees, fruity,
Hedges also laden with booty.

Trees are bare,
Winter's almost here.

Mark Libby (9)
Ingleby Arncliffe CE Primary School

What Am I?

I can cover the ground in fifteen minutes flat
And cause a great blizzard
You can jump in me and play in me
You can make a snowman out of me
When you touch me, I am soft but
Very cold
I can cover the whole world, white
When I am angry, I can block you in your house.
So what am I?

Rebecca Marsden (10)
Ingleby Arncliffe CE Primary School

Gathering Leaves

G athering the autumn leaves,
A fter they have fallen.
T he leaves, floating down like feathers.
H ooray, it's time for autumn,
E veryone enjoying the fun,
R unning till the day is done.
I n the rain and in the sun,
N ever stopping, always going
G reat, great fun.

L ovely colours blending in,
E ach and everyone unique,
A nd the dry leaves crisp out, as
V ast veins spread out.
E arthy smells,
S ee you next year, autumn leaves.

Charity Cornforth (9)
Ingleby Arncliffe CE Primary School

Autumn

The piles of leaves as big as towers
And all the bright colours of the flowers.

All the animals waking in the morning
Listening to the birds, new dawning.

The berries being picked, leaving red marks on your hands,
The farmers getting ready to plough their lands.

The morning has come and
The sun rises on the juicy plums.

Emily Kitching (9)
Ingleby Arncliffe CE Primary School

Bogeyman

My parents used to tell me
When I was a wee boy
That if I didn't go to sleep
The bogeyman would get me!
His face was red
His eyes were green,
His nose was blue
He was very mean.
I couldn't go to sleep at night
Because he would give me a fright.
Well, that was earlier
And this is the way
I've learned my lesson . . .
I'm wiser today.

Joshua Meyer (10)
Longman's Hill CP School

My Dad's A Monster

My dad's a monster
It has been said
I'm sure he lurks under my bed
And then at night, outside he creeps
Just to make sure that I'm fast asleep.

But when I wake for another day
And say, 'Come on Dad, it's time to play.'
He runs around with my football
Perhaps he's not so bad, after all.

Until he tackles me to the ground
And jumps about with a whooping sound,
He's so determined to get the ball
That *he is* a monster, after all!

Sam Gill (10)
Longman's Hill CP School

The Bedroom Monster

'There's no monsters,' said Dad.

Noises in the cupboard
Movement all around
Creaking from the floorboards
Shadows making figures.

Cupboard doors opening
Creaking all the time,
Shadows running mad
All through the night.
Toys making noises
Creeping me out!

Moon flickers through
Lights go out
Thumping downstairs
Might be the monster,
Getting Mum and Dad.
What shall I do?
Go downstairs
Or will the monster get me
Or shall I go to sleep?

Monsters come out now
I am asleep,
Creeping outside
Slamming the door.

The monsters are gone
I am awake,
Creeping little sounds
In my head.

I have to go to sleep
Before the monster attacks.

Joshua Oliver (11)
Longman's Hill CP School

The Monster

There is a monster in my wardrobe,
There is a monster in my clothes,
There is a monster in my bed!

There is a monster under my bed.
Dad said,
There is a monster in my head.

There is a monster on my chair,
There is a monster on my drawers,
There is a monster on my bed.

He is spotty,
He is dotty,
He is scary!

He is blue,
He is black,
He is darey!

He is wet,
He is dry,
He is hairy!

He is in my head,
Daddy said.
But he is scary!

The monster is scary!
The monster is darey!
The monster is hairy!

'There is a monster under my bed,' I said
But I know he is in my head!

Alice Priddy (10)
Longman's Hill CP School

Paint The Bedroom Blue

Paint the bedroom blue,
It's really cool
Please, paint the bedroom blue!

Paint the table,
Paint the bed,
Paint the chair,
Paint my hair.
It's really scary at night
I always want to turn on the light.

There's monsters, snakes and dreads,
They all sleep under my bed.
They sleep in the day and come out at night,
Just waiting to give me a fright.

Listen, listen, please do ,
Don't go into my bedroom
I don't want them to get you too!

They've got my teddies, Ping and Pong,
They've been gone for very long.

'Who's got your teddies?' my mum said.
'The monsters that live under my bed,' I said!

Rebecca Meir (10)
Longman's Hill CP School

Creak

Once my dad told me there were monsters
under my bed - are there?

I dreamt of it tickling me, picking me up
and throwing me.
It's big brown beady eyes staring at me,
It's big and hairy, purple and blue.

My bed goes
Creak . . . creak . . . creak!

Emma Noble (10)
Longman's Hill CP School

The Ice Queen

Inside, it's warm
But outside it's cold,
This is my ice room
I think I've found mould!

I won't touch my cupboard,
Because the Ice Queen will come,
I can't hold my breath
So instead I just hum.

I can't get to sleep
It's the fourth time this week.
I'm laid on my bed
With thoughts in my head.

I can hear tapping
I think it's my mum.
I can hear scratching
My hands have gone numb.

I hear her coming,
Slipping and sliding,
I'm under my covers
Because I am hiding.

I can't get to sleep,
It's the fourth time this week.
I'm laid on my bed
With thoughts in my head.

She's scary
She's hairy,

She's dotty
She's spotty.

I'm not scared of the Ice Queen,
Because she's gone, without being seen.

Lauren Gouldsbrough (10)
Longman's Hill CP School

Mum, It's Not Fair!

'Mum, it's not fair, I want to cut my hair,
Every time I want something
You never seem to care.'

'Mum, it's not fair
Eliza's cut her hair,
I don't see why I can't
It's just not fair.'

'You can have some pens in a pack,
But if you don't stop moaning
I'll give you a smack.'

My mum's not fair
She buys stuff for herself
She never seems to notice me
She won't even buy me a shelf.

It's like I'm not real
I feel like a piece of mud
I've got a plan but it might fail,
You never know, it could turn out good.

I sneak in the room where she's watching TV
I sneak into her purse
Sshh! This is between you and me.

'And what do you think you're doing,
Scrounging in my purse?'
Sooo you wear my socks . . . ?
That's even worse!
'You're grounded!'

That's the end of me!

Lauren Darley (10)
Longman's Hill CP School

Mummy . . . Help!

I was in my bed
I saw a big ted,
I heard a creak
I thought it was a squeak!
'Mummy . . . help!'

I went under my cover
I saw something hover,
It was white
And camouflaged in the night.
'Mummy . . . help!'

I felt something on me
I had to look up.
I saw something on my chair
I hid under the covers
And messed with my hair.
'Mummy . . . help!'

I felt really scared
Someone turned on the light.
'Mummy, is that you?' I said
I looked up in the night.
'M . . . Mummy . . . help!'

'What's the matter dear?' she said.
'Mummy, it's you! There's a monster
under my bed.'

I slept for hours then there was a squeak.
'Mummy . . . help!'

Amy Richardson (10)
Longman's Hill CP School

Creepers

There's no monsters under your bed,
I locked them all up in the shed.
If you don't go to sleep
Out they come and they will creep!

You never went to sleep last night,
They're coming to give you a fright.
Shadows move on the walls
You can hear whispered calls,
The calls are coming from the north side
I go under the covers, try and hide.

The shadows have gone from the room,
This might be time for my doom!
The only light in the room
Is the sparkling twinkle from the moon.

The monsters are coming for me,
It's time for breakfast, dinner and tea.
I shut my eyes
The sun will rise and
It's morning!

Jordan Davy (10)
Longman's Hill CP School

The Devil In My Cupboard

I won't come out, the Devil is near
I've been a girl, I'm safe in here.
You're horrible, wet, red and mean
Don't come near me, please oh please!
You've hurt me enough,
Please can I come out?
I'll tell my daddy,
Go away now!

Lydia Ross (9)
Longman's Hill CP School

Creeping Monster

A monster could be creeping
When I'm sleeping,
Hiding under my bed
That's what my dad said.

It could be greedy
It might eat me.
What if it takes me
Then it bakes me
(Ready for its Sunday dinner).

It could come through the window,
The cupboard
The door
Worst, my bed
Argh!

Best go to sleep now
I hope I'm dreaming
A monster could be creeping
When I'm sleeping.
Hiding under my bed
That's what my dad said.

Joel Vickers (10)
Longman's Hill CP School

Jungle

Lion's roar, give me its paw
Monkeys swang, I grew a fang.
Birds fly - that looks a great pie!
Elephants stand - they look grand!
Spiders crawl, let's go to the Mall!
Snakes hiss, that's a near miss!

Mark Dickinson (11)
Longman's Hill CP School

The Garden Path . . .

The garden path twists and turns . . .
The trees rustle their leaves in the gentle breeze.

The plants dance in the wind . . .
The grass plays a tune.

The greenhouse is silent inside . . .
The plants are still like soldiers in a row.

The pond ripples in the breeze . . .
The birds sing in a group.

The swing is slowly swinging
Back and forth in the wind
Silent . . . silent . . .
As can be . . .

Now we must leave . . .
The garden is at peace . . .

The garden was mine!

Laura Stephenson (11)
Longman's Hill CP School

Bad Hair Day!

I looked in the mirror
And to my dread
I saw that horns
Had sprung from my head!

My friends in class
Were angry all day,
They couldn't see the teacher
Because my horns were in the way!

The teacher was angry,
He started to yell,
It was maybe because
I'd used too much gel!

Jaymie Welsh-Richardson (11)
Longhman's Hill CP School

Sitting In Maths Thinking Of Something To Do!

The bell rang for the end of playtime,
I came marching in.

I came into the classroom still
marching past the bin.

I sat down in my comfy chair,
took out my book and pen.

Then waited for the teacher to come
and to count from ten . . .
10, 9, 8 . . .

The lesson soon began
The teacher's voice droned on.

Putting crosses in my book . . .
Wrong! Wrong! Wrong!

Becki Stubbs (9)
Longman's Hill CP School

The Giant Clock

Tick-tock, tick-tock!
Oh no! It's that giant clock
My dad said in the clock, a monster will creep
And grab my legs when I'm asleep.
I've opened that big door
Once before.
In the clock there was a giant croc
With one eye.
I hide in my bed and tried not to cry.
Tick-tock, tick-tock!
Oh no! It's that giant clock.

Conor Hoop (10)
Longman's Hill CP School

Silly Mum

'Goodnight Sweetheart!
Don't let the bed bugs bite!'
Here I am shivering with fright.
Will the bed bugs really bite?

I wonder what are bed bugs?
Maybe they're alien-like thugs!
Do they really bite?
I thought with fright.

It's strange you know,
I've looked and looked
But I can't find any -
Maybe they're invisible or it's just pure lies.

I don't believe Mum anymore
I'm just itchy and horribly sore,
Honestly, some people are nuts
Ouch! I've been bitten!

Natalie Wiles (10)
Longman's Hill CP School

The Day Humpty Dumpty Fell Off The Wall

The day Humpty Dumpty fell off the wall
Little Bo Peep lost her sheep.
Jack and Jill went up the hill,
Mary's lamb disrupted the school.
Baa Baa Black Sheep lost his wool!
Hey Diddle Diddle stole the cat's fiddle,
The cow had eaten the moon.
The dog had choked laughing
The dish ran away with the spoon
And then . . .
They all went to help Humpty Dumpty!

Jess Piercy (10)
Longman's Hill CP School

Mummy! Mummy . . . Help!

'Mummy! Mummy help! There's a mmm . . . *monster!*
And it's gonna get me!'
One night before I went to sleep my Dad told me . . .
'Go to sleep! Or the monster will come!'

Now I dream of creepy things
With one eye, two or even three!
Now I'm scared. Whenever someone walks past . . .
'Mummy! Mummy . . . help!'

I quickly run to turn the light on, but it was only my mum.
'What's the matter?' she said.
'There's a monster . . . a real monster! It's got a green eye
and yellow skin with purple spots upon his chin!
Honest!'

Then I heard a monster noise, it was coming from
my brother's bedroom!
'Mummy! Mummy, help . . . Josh!
But it was only his PlayStation and game!
Now I'm ten and older now.
I don't believe in monsters!

Katy Gibbon (10)
Longman's Hill CP School

Inspiration

I can't make up poems
Because they don't rhyme
I know you don't have to make them rhyme
But it can make a difference.
I asked my mum if she could help me
But she said in a sorry voice,
'I'm no use, I can't make-up poems!'
So I sat there all day, trying to think
Of something when all of a sudden . . .
I've got it - inspiration!

Rachel Horsman (10)
Longman's Hill CP School

The Jungle Bedroom

My bedroom's really messy
And I really need to sleep.
I'm in a jungle bedroom
That I've made up this week.

My jumper's hanging off the radio,
It looks just like a monkey.
I'm in a jungle bedroom
And it's really funky.

There's a walking pair of shoes
I'm sure they were hedgehogs.
I'm in a jungle bedroom
And I'm standing on a log.

It's night-time in the jungle,
Out of the dark.
Comes the jungle spiders,
They give me a start,

The sun is rising.
The crocs are snapping,
I'm in a jungle bedroom
And Mummy's tapping.
'Get that bedroom cleaned up
or I'll set the lions on you.'

Shauna Abbott (10)
Longman's Hill CP School

Mummy There's A Monster Under My Bed!

Last night when I was fast asleep,
I heard a terrible creak.
It sounded like a mouse, sharpening his teeth.
'Mummy, there's a monster under my bed!'

I hid under the covers
And saw shadows dancing round my room.
'Mummy there's a monster under my bed!'

I looked up from my covers and saw . . .
My baby sister on the floor.
'Mummy there's a monster on the floor!'

Sarah Latteman (11)
Longman's Hill CP School

Nonsense Poem About My Brother

My boring stupid brother
Always hangs round with my mother.
He never wants to play with me,
Unless it's climbing up a tree!
Of course, he plays out with his friends
And his friendship never ends.
I'm happy for him, most of the time,
But playing with me, he thinks it's a crime!

Laura Hodgkiss (10)
Long Preston Primary School

Hamtarrow

I've got a hamster
Who lives in a cage
Hamtarrow is his name

He's two years old
And likes to play
But never runs away

Unlike me
He eats nuts and seeds
And stuffs it in his pouch

He keeps it there
Then takes it to his lair
And eats it for his lunch

There's just no doubt
He's a good friend
And will always be there.

Oliver Robinson (9)
Long Preston Primary School

My Poem

Cows in the fields
Cows being milked
Cows having meals
Cows everywhere.

Sheep in the sheds
Sheep in the fields
Sheep in bed
Sheep everywhere.

Pigs in the mud
Pigs in the sty
(But pigs can't fly!)
Pigs everywhere!

Daniel F Thompson (7)
Long Preston Primary School

Sleepover Chick

When I go to sleepovers
I never get to sleep
We go and peep over
My little sister's door
To see if she's asleep!

Eleanor Coultherd (9)
Long Preston Primary School

Dragons

Long ago when dragons ruled the Earth
Like kings up in the air
In the ancient valleys deep
They dwell down in their lair
But they also fly up in the sky
Like gallant gulls up high
Bold warriors face the beast but flee at first glance
Long ago when dragons ruled the Earth
Lost in the reign of fire.

Alexander Cardwell (10)
Long Preston Primary School

The Yorkshire Dales

The little village below the hill,
Hiding behind the enormous mill.
Flowers fill up all the fields, green,
Cottages, the prettiest ever seen.

Joseph Clark (7)
Long Preston Primary School

Lambing Time

Early hours of the morning
You walk onto the farm,
At first the land seems quiet
And everything is calm.

Then you walk into the field
And there they all lay,
Lots of tiny little lambs
Perfect in every way.

But then you see a lamb that's lame,
I rush to get my dad.
He comes right away
To give it a life-saving jab.

Stephanie Thompson (10)
Long Preston Primary School

The Bossy Young Tree

'Fallen leaves,' said the tree
'Are merely debris.
Do ask the wind
To blow them away.'

'Before a year can pass
They will rot into me
So don't be an ass!'
Said the grass.

Nancy Marchesi (10)
Long Preston Primary School

Space

Space is an ocean of black
To stick to the ground use Blu-tack
A big, wide, vast, dark place
There before the human race
A great, big, bright, white moon
It rises and falls in the gloom
Huge hot sun shines bright
But disappears again in the night.

Michael Moon (8)
Long Preston Primary School

I Stood And Saw

I stood and saw the green grass swaying from side to side,
The shops standing straight in a row.
The Market Cross In the middle of the town, all alone.
The Village Hall with the prize-winning toilets next door.

I stood and heard the birds singing happily in the trees,
The church bells ringing, the toilets flushing,
The wind howling loudly and people laughing and talking.

I stood and smelled the fish and chips firing up for tea,
The smell of the beer from all the pubs,
The smell of air pollution coming from the cars.
The fresh, country air.

I stood and felt the rough stone on the Market Cross,
The wood on the benches,
The metal posts holding the sign

Kimberly Jayne Alderson (10)
Mill Hill CP School

Old People

Soft, dry hands
Always cold,
Help needed
They say
Respect your elders.

If you do, you will be respected.
Listen to them,
I am sure they're right.
They overload you with sweets and
They're kind to you so be
Kind to them.

Samantha Ross (9)
Mill Hill CP School

A Happy Face

All around me, all I see are happy faces
Smiling at me
Would you want a happy face?
If so, join the race!
There's one for everyone, you know
So don't be low
So don't be slow.

I know one thing and it's
That I can bring a . . .
Happy, happy, face.

Natalie Gardiner (11)
Mill Hill CP School

Grandad

Grandad I love you
And I always will,
In both the summer
And in the chill.

But I know I will always
Have you in my heart,
When I am feeling happy
And when I am feeling like
I am falling apart.

Christina Stephenson (10)
Mill Hill CP School

Vast

I'd rather be on the ground than fall,
I'd rather be a scarf than a shawl.
I'd rather be at home than at the mall,
I'd rather be a message than a call,
I'd rather be a shop than a stall.
I'd rather be a train set than a ball,
I'd rather be short than tall.
I'd rather be here than not at all.

Molly Parker & Levon Barkhordarian (10)
Newby & Scalby Primary School

The Snow Is Wonderful

Snow is bright,
Cold, cold white,
People play in the
White, sparkly, twinkling snow.

George Allen (7)
Newby & Scalby Primary School

I'd Rather Be Free

I'd rather be honey than a bee,
I'd rather be a door than a key,
I'd rather be a golf ball than a tee,
I'd rather be a dog than a flea.
I'd rather be the sand than the sea,
I'd rather be a leaf than a tree,
I'd rather demand than plea,
But most of all, I'd like to be free!

Andrew Bryant & Sophie Smith (10)
Newby & Scalby Primary School

Gentle Snow

Gentle snow comes down gently
So gentle, you can't even feel it
Building a snowman is relaxing
Putting the carrot and stones on it
In the night
Watching over the snowflakes and
I squelch my snowman and the snowflakes.

Leah Sue-Ann Harrison (8)
Newby & Scalby Primary School

The Snowman

I went outside and saw a man
Who was covered in snow.
I was shivering, as cold as ever
I was so scared, I ran to the door.
But then I noticed that the man
Covered in snow, didn't move.
It was called a snowman, because
It was made of snow.

Stacy Ness (7)
Newby & Scalby Primary School

Trust

Friends are always loyal
Trust's honest and has reliability.
It never betrays you or anyone
Your family always keeps a secret
And stands beside you.
Some people, it turns out, are unreliable
I take responsibility for lies,
Alistair's a faithful supporter of Leeds Utd
And so is Luke to some extent . . .
Which to him is a complement.

Alex Lenton (9)
Newby & Scalby Primary School

Snow

Snow falls fast to the ground
Over the fields, snow falls.
Wet snow falls to the ground,
Flakes are white.
Let us see the snowman,
And when you touch it, it is cold.
Kicking noises were coming down from the sky,
Every morning, snow is still there.

Emma Botham (8)
Newby & Scalby Primary School

Ice

I'm sacrificing
I'm sacrificing
I am ice
I am so cold.
I glisten when the sun comes out,
And when you stand on me
I'm like a biscuit.

Jacquetta Johnson (8)
Newby & Scalby Primary School

Snow

The snow was falling very fast,
So I went outside and
Built a snowman.
On the ground
It was icy and frosty.
Then I saw a snowball.
One, then two, then three, then four
Then five, then six.

Gabrielle J Flockton (7)
Newby & Scalby Primary School

Five Little Snowflakes

As the snow falls down,
The boy throws snowballs at the ground
But then one little snowflake falls down.
Then two, then three, then four, then five
As we clear them off the drive.

Jamie Muirhead (8)
Newby & Scalby Primary School

Snow

You can play
You can lie in the snow
You can make cold snowballs
You can throw cold snowballs
You can get hit by a snowball
You can skid
You can make snowmen and
You can make angels.

Michael Tindall (7)
Newby & Scalby Primary School

One Little Snowflake

Crunch, brrr!
Falling, quickly, silently, glittering, snowboarding, cold.

One little snowflake fluttering down, falling, slowly
Landing silently on a boy.
The boy yelled, 'Brrrr! That's freezing!'
And ran inside as fast as his legs could take him
To warm up.

Nathan Corden (8)
Newby & Scalby Primary School

Snow Falling

There was not a sound, not even a mouse could be heard
Then there it was - falling down onto the ground with a loud plop.
I ran out with my hat, scarf and gloves and put my coat on.
I stuck my tongue out at it, it was cold.
It was sparkly and shiny, I loved it
It was snow falling.

Nicole Chapman (8)
Newby & Scalby Primary School

Snow

Snow is like a blanket that covers everywhere,
You take it in your hand and throw it in the air.

When you stand on snow, it crunches like a crisp,
It might hurt your hand, so hit it with your fist.

Alexander Kirk (8)
Newby & Scalby Primary School

Snow

I woke up, I was surprised to see the
grass was covered with something.
I asked my mum, but she said
Nothing, then I asked my dad,
He said nothing as well!

So I went outside and I was shivering
To death, like an ice cube.
I picked up a lump and made a hard ball
Then threw it. *Splat!* It said and then
I knew that it was snow!

Ione Wells (8)
Newby & Scalby Primary School

Snow

Snow sparkles like a diamond,
No school today, it is shut.
Over the clouds, there is the sun.
We went sledding.
Building a snowman.
Laughing because of the snow.
A boy is hurt because of the snow
Kicking a ball of snow.
Everyone is having fun.

Emily James (8)
Newby & Scalby Primary School

Falling Snow

Snow is soft, fluffy and cold
Snow is as white as a cloud
Melts slowly in the sun
When the moon comes up
It snows and falls again.

Maddy Wood (7)
Newby & Scalby Primary School

Snowflake

Snow is like a blanket, it covers everywhere.
You take it in your hand and throw it in the air and then
It gives you hypothermia.

When you stand on snowflakes, they crunch
Like a biscuit when you eat it.
It looks like a glass of water when you drink it.

Euan David Riby (7)
Newby & Scalby Primary School

The White Snow

Snowflakes fall while children play,
Play in the crispy, crunchy snow.
They build an angry snowman
The bright sun is its energy because it
Makes the shining snow.
Then the snow is gone for ever.

Chrisopher Holmes (7)
Newby & Scalby Primary School

Winter Is Now

Sun, sun, come with me
I want it to be warm.
Now look outside at the snow
Winter is *now!*

Adele Swift (7)
Newby & Scalby Primary School

Bug Chant

Red bugs, head bugs
Lousy little dead bugs

Kink bugs, link bugs
Hiding with the Sphinx bugs

Eye bugs, sly bugs
Eating all the pie bugs

Flea bugs, glee bugs
Climbing up your knee bugs

Floor bugs, door bugs
Always wanting more bugs

Air bugs, flare bugs
Always everywhere bugs

Quick bugs, slick bugs
Playing crafty tricks bugs

Glow bugs, slow bugs
Find them with your toe bugs

Shoe bugs, flu bugs
Like the word cuckoo bugs

Drive bugs, dive bugs
Going to a hive bugs

Time bugs, rhyme bugs
Like to eat your lime bugs

Buzzzzz!

Andrew Howson (9)
Newby & Scalby Primary School

Snowman Power Of Glory

Snow is not slippery, ice is
Snow floats on water, ice drops
Some people like snow.

Matthew Richings (7)
Newby & Scalby Primary School

Winter World

When I woke up one frosty morning,
And heard the sound of church bells.
I ran downstairs to get breakfast ready,
I looked out of the frozen window to see
A thick white, blanket.
Guess what it was?
Snow!

Chloe Merritt (7)
Newby & Scalby Primary School

New Year Day

It's gleaming white,
It's fluffy as a cloud
It's cold as ice
It's slippy as ice,
It's *snow!*

Abhishek NG (7)
Newby & Scalby Primary School

Snow

S now is bright and brilliant
N oisy hailstones hit the window
O ver the mountains they skid
W hite, shiny, gleaming snow.

Amber-Rose McCrory (7)
Newby & Scalby Primary School

Mount Everest

I'm climbing
up Mount Everest
Mount Everest is snow,
is snow. Mount Everest is tall
and big and even gigantic, but
most of all, it's got snow.

I'm sliding
down Mount Everest
Mount Everest is snow,
is snow. Mount Everest is tall
and big and even gigantic but
most of all, it's got snow.

Thomas Heaton (7)
Newby & Scalby Primary School

My Sister In Winter

As it floats gently to the ground, my sister
is singing Jinglebells and dancing all around.

When it settles on the garden floor, my sister
knocks down her bedroom door.

When it's winter I nearly scream as my sister
makes the snow into an ice cream
And she makes me eat it too!

Thomas Broughton (7)
Newby & Scalby Primary School

I Looked Out My Window . . .

I looked out my window, guess what I saw?
Icicles dangling
To and fro
Snow falling
On the floor.

Steven Broadbent (7)
Newby & Scalby Primary School

Snow

It was a cold, icy day
The garden was covered in a white duvet.
Flakes of white were falling down, down.
White creamy-coloured men were dancing,
Dancing to the wind.
When I looked even harder, I saw they were snowmen
And that the duvet was snow!

Megan Woodward-Hay (7)
Newby & Scalby Primary School

The Snow

It was a cold, cold day
When it was snowing.
The ice was slippy and skiddy.
The garden was like a baby's blanket
When the footprints walked on the cold floor
The footprints were tempted to walk.

Georgiana Swalwell Pashby (7)
Newby & Scalby Primary School

Flowers

Daisies, daffodils
Lots and lots of cheerful ones
Swaying in the breeze
They are all so beautiful
Reflecting in the sunshine.

Sophie Williams (8)
Newby & Scalby Primary School

Alliteration

One orange obediently ordered
Two turtles talked till ten o'clock
Three thumbs thought about thorns
Four foreign Furbies flew to Florida
Five fat figs figured out five plus five
Six stupid singers sweetly sang.
Seven slimy snakes sat on Sophie's seat,
Eight elephants eat eggs every eighty days
Nine naughts nuts nastily nipped nice nuns
Ten tuneful tigers tangoed to the tune.

Jessica Donnelly (9)
Newby & Scalby Primary School

A Bug Chant

Slow bugs, low bugs
Tickling in your toe bugs

Big bugs, small bugs,
Some very heavy bugs

Floor bugs, more bugs,
And I've got four bugs

Hairy bugs, silly bugs,
And some really bold bugs.

Harmony Hudgell (8)
Newby & Scalby Primary School

Winter

Snowballs in the air,
Icicles hanging, dripping,
People make snowmen
Snowploughs clearing paths,
Snowflakes falling from the sky.

Nick Perry (8)
Newby & Scalby Primary School

Roses

Beautiful roses
Flowers growing everywhere
Pink, yellow, red, white
In soil which is fertile
Fantastic smell from all kinds.

Tzarini Meyler (8)
Newby & Scalby Primary School

Summer

The sun shines brightly
The plants sway in the light wind,
You go out to play
People go out to the beach.

Adam Newbould (8)
Newby & Scalby Primary School

Haiku Poem

Funny guinea pig
Cute cuddly consuming cat
Restless round rabbit.

David Shaw (8)
Newby & Scalby Primary School

A Bug Poem

Flat bugs, thin bugs,
Anywhere in your hair bugs

Tall bugs, small bugs,
Standing on you wall bugs

Smart bugs, thick bugs,
Crawling in your cream bugs

Caring bugs, daring bugs
Jumping on your head bugs

Light bugs, night bugs
Going in your pants bugs.

Daniel Petty (9)
Newby & Scalby Primary School

Bug Poems

Slimy bugs, creepy bugs,
Little scrappy baby bugs.

Eye bugs, pie bugs,
Little juicy adult bugs.

Trick bugs, flip bugs,
Little squashed floor bugs.

Green bugs, yellow bugs,
Swimming in your drink bugs.

Katie Hastie (8)
Newby & Scalby Primary School

Bug Dance

On the night of the bug dance
The bugs went wild
The bug was doing the hand jive.

As soon as the bug band started to play
The flies were flying the wrong way
So can we play all day, yeah?

It's time to eat to the boogie beat
The moths are having a great big treat
So that's the end of the boogie beat.

So let's give a cheer for the big boogie bugs!

Katy Millions (9)
Newby & Scalby Primary School

Winter Haiku

Icicles spiky
White snow falling from the sky
Snowballs all over.

Connor Greenhough (8)
Newby & Scalby Primary School

Parents

I like my parents
Because they wash my clothes
They help me with maths

They play with me all day long and
They let me watch television.

Anannyua Kumarvel (8)
Newby & Scalby Primary School

Bug Poem

Slimy bugs, hairy bugs, racing down
your hair bugs,

Big bugs, small bugs, wiggling in your
sock bugs.

Scarab bugs, creepy bugs, coming in
your body bugs,

Stinging bugs, crunchy bugs, killing
body bugs.

Ben Allison (8)
Newby & Scalby Primary School

Panther

P ounces when hunting
A ggressive when annoyed
N ever white
T all and strong
H ates it when they don't catch food
E xtremely black in colour
R oooaaaar!

Nell Baker (8)
Newby & Scalby Primary School

Summer On The Mountain

Summer on the mountain
Picking billberries by the ton
A light breeze is blowing
The sea ripples below
Summer on the mountain.

Laura Davidson (8)
Newby & Scalby Primary School

Bug Chant

Squashy bugs, thin bugs,
Find them in the ear bugs.

Green bugs, fat bugs,
Find them in the ear bugs.

String bugs, baby bugs,
Find them in the ear bugs.

Flicky bugs, slicky bugs
Find them in the ear bugs.

Slime bugs, pie bugs,
Find them in the knee bugs.

Eye bugs, fly bugs
Find them in the house bugs.

Ginger bugs, blue bugs,
Find them in the nose bugs.

Soft bugs, red bugs,
Find them in the back bugs.

Samantha Greenham (8)
Newby & Scalby Primary School

People

Some people are big, some people are small
Some are short and some are tall
But I know the best person of all
And she's called Emily Hampton
She loves a bit of Paddington
He's so sweet and strong
I love people most of all.

Jordan Kelly (8)
Newby & Scalby Primary School

Bug Chant

Floor bugs, more bugs,
Nasty little floor bugs

Red bugs, yellow bugs
Mean little red bugs

Wine bugs, slime bugs
Nasty little knee bugs

Black bugs, slack bugs
Mean little buzz bugs

Silly bugs, loopy bugs
Find them in your circus bugs.

Sam Ellwood (9)
Newby & Scalby Primary School

Seasons

Spring is colourful
Autumn is brown and crunchy,
Winter is wonderful
Summer is hot and happy.
All the seasons are great.

Spring is warm,
Autumn is crunchy leaves,
Winter is cold,
Summer is picnics and games
All the seasons are great.

Hollie Rowe (9)
Newby & Scalby Primary School

A River's Life

When I started young and free,
My mind was racing like traffic in the rush hour,
Eroding as I charged furiously down the ice-capped mountain,
Crashing, rough - made of strong currents was I.

I reached the valley
More gently and docile
But still eroding.
Getting wider from confluences,
Passing floodplains,
I came to a jogging pace
Starting to deposit.

Reaching grass plains,
If seen, bliss!
I was steady like a tortoise, looking for a lettuce leaf,
Passing villages, towns, cities
Meandering calmly,
Flowing, trickling, quiet was I.
Children splashing in my path.

Soon after my journey ended at a lake,
And all was still.

Eilish McCausland (11)
Newby & Scalby Primary School

Bumps

Things that go bump in the night
Gave Susie White a fright.
She saw a ghost eating jam
In a big, red van.

Daniel Riley (8)
Newby & Scalby Primary School

Untitled

Elephants are big
Dogs can go woof
    Cats can go miaow
    Skunks are stinky
    And so is muddy grass.

Sweets are chewy
Flowers are colourful
    Biscuits are yummy
    Like brown and white chocolate
    But sweet laces are the best.

Animals walking on the street,
Animals walking in the town,
There is none in the zoo
But we want there to be.

Connor Ramsden (8)
Newby & Scalby Primary School

Weather

Rain weeps buckets, as the clouds turn grey,
Storm clouds gather and leave behind the day.
Lightning races across the sky,
Thunder laughs evilly, no one knows why!

Snow, it falls and hits the ground,
Wind, it whistles and moves around.
Hail flies and hits your face,
Tornado hurries and wins the race.

Sun is calming, warm and kind
And happy thoughts, they fill her mind
And when she shines the whole world sees
All the Earth's natural beauties.

Ellie Hornsby (10)
Newby & Scalby Primary School

A River

As a youth, high up in a towering mountain
It wildly erupts and gushes down,
Rapidly it roughly tears at the sopping bank
Viciously crushing rocks and boulders in its way.
As furious as a lion
As fast as a gazelle.

Now at working pace, it steadily flows
From the mountain to the valley.
Dropping the boulders picked up earlier.
Slowed, but not stopped.
Curving through the valley
Pushing onwards.

Now the river begins to loiter,
Relaxing, spreading over the plain.
Hugely tedious, as slothful as ever.
Speed all ceased, a meandering tortoise,
Then it reaches the sea.

Frederick Jackson (10)
Newby & Scalby Primary School

The Bumpily Bump

Things that go bump in the night
Sure to get a fright, the floorboards are
Creaking and the cat's miaowing
Windows smashing, footsteps
Standing on the floor.
Beware of bugles.

Mark Thompson (8)
Newby & Scalby Primary School

River Poem

Water came spilling down the
Rocky snow-capped mountain
Like wild horses galloping in the snow
Rushing left and right into the valley.

Down into the deep valley, gurgling
On over pebbles and rocks
Rushing forwards carrying on to its new life.

Out on the wide open plain standing
Still and silent
Calm and gently resting in the sunlight
Journey over.

Lucy Tindall (10)
Newby & Scalby Primary School

River's Poem

Malicious river crashing hastily down the snow-capped mountain,
Grinding into rocks taking them away like a dog biting into a bone.
Waterfall crashing down pouring to the ground, as fast as a shark
catching prey.

Comes to the valley of river and starts to jog like a man getting tired
in a race.

Comes to the plain and starts to slow down as slow as a tortoise,
It gets further down and starts to meander like a snake bending
round a tree,
It gracefully flows like a swan to the end and meets up with the sea.

Luke Botham (10)
Newby & Scalby Primary School

Rivers

Malicious river, galloping down the snow-capped
Mountain, like a beautiful white stallion.

Cascading evil river, crashing down the steep rocky
Mountain, picking up boulders like they were feathers.

Jogging river, meandering through the peaceful valley,
the stallion has slowed to a canter.

Trickling river, flowing through the grassy plain,
The stallion has finished the race.

Sophie Ness (11)
Newby & Scalby Primary School

Concorde River

Boisterous river,
Flows as fast as Concorde,
At supersonic speed.

Crashes over rough rocks,
Forms a mini waterfall.

Slowly drifting along
Like an old ant with one leg gone.

Very slowly like a snail in pain.

Alex Walker (10)
Newby & Scalby Primary School

Trust

I believe you, you wild boy!
As you are my most loyal knight
And you are a true friend
You really are reliable, aren't you?
That was unbelievable, wasn't it lads?
You are very trusting.

Andrew Trigg (9)
Newby & Scalby Primary School

A River's Journey

Boisterously the angry waters rapidly flowed down the rugged
mountain, eroding to the next part of the river.

The easy waters were briskly flowing down the sloping valley,
depositing rocks as it runs to the relaxed plains.

Peacefully the water meandered, tediously loitering, down
the tranquil plain.

Emily Doveton (11)
Newby & Scalby Primary School

A Poem About A River

Erupting boisterous river, crashing down ice snow-capped mountain
like lava from an active volcano spilling over jagged rocks.
River descending slows its mad dash, passing through.
Valleys dropping all it carries to the river bed but
Still mud and pebbles go on their journey until the river halts.

Tom Newlove
Newby & Scalby Primary School

River

Erupting, boisterous, zooming through the Rocky Mountains,
Gushing swiftly through the depths of the valleys
Meeting tributaries along the way.
The soft eroded rock banks glistening in the sun.

The smell of the salt not far away,
The end of the journey at the end of the day.

Robert Wilson (11)
Newby & Scalby Primary School

River Poem

Malicious, rapid pounding river, running away
From the mountain source.
Picking up pebbles and rocks as it erodes away
huge mountain rocks.
Then a waterfall babbles along then skips into the valley.
It meanders down through the small village
Into a slow tortoise style speed
Then it just relaxes.

Niall Gibb (10)
Newby & Scalby Primary School

Trust

I rely on my friends,
I tell them all my secrets.
They keep them to themselves,
They never lie to me.
I never lie to them
They ring me every night
And I trust them a hundred percent.

Hanna Larrson (10)
Newby & Scalby Primary School

Trust

I rely on doctors and nurses
I depend on my riding teacher
My friends are loyal to me
My mum and dad can keep secrets
Truth is what people like
I promise I'll look after people
My friends have faith in me.

Mollie Graham (10)
Newby & Scalby Primary School

Trust

My family is kind and helpful
My friends are loyal to me,
I'm friendly with all my friends,
I tell the truth to my dad
My mum is kind to me.
My doctor is honest with me
My dad is kind to me
My family is very truthful.
I believe in my family and
I trust my good friend, Olivia.

Amy Watkin (9)
Newby & Scalby Primary School

Trust

My friends are kind to me,
My friends are loyal to me.
My friends are trustworthy and kind,
My friends can keep a secret.
I trust my friends to keep my secrets,
I trust my friend called Alex.
My friends help me when I am hurt.

Stephen Gaines (10)
Newby & Scalby Primary School

Trust

I believed in my brother
I thought he would keep my secret
I had trusted him!
The next day he told my friend
I talked to my friend -
He said he would keep my secret.

Mark Jackson (10)
Newby & Scalby Primary School

Trust

My friends, all of them
I never have any doubt about them
They're kind and special to me.
They drive me round the bend
But are always trustworthy friends.
I have an awful lot of them and they're
Always honest with me.
I have faith in them,
They have faith in me.

Tiffany Rowe (9)
Newby & Scalby Primary School

Trust

I trust my friend Matthew Prince
I'm trusting of my friends.
My friends are faithful to my mum and me,
My friends can keep a secret,
I help people with their work.
My friends rely on me
My friends are dependable to me.
I'm honest with my friends.

Matthew Gibson (9)
Newby & Scalby Primary School

Trust

My friends will tell the truth,
I trust my doctor, he's trustworthy.
I trust my family, they're faithful
Joe will tell the truth - not!
Luke is sort of honest,
I am honest, sort of!
My teacher wouldn't lie to me.
My family are loyal to me,
My cousin is faithful
You're honest and kind to me.

Alistair Haythorne (9)
Newby & Scalby Primary School

Trust

I believe my friend James
He's my best friend, I can trust him
He will keep my secret
I can believe him until I die
If he's hurt, I will believe him and help him
I will believe him forever
We will be best friends forever
If he tells me his secret -
I won't tell anyone!
Just like he won't tell my secret.

Adam Umpleby (9)
Newby & Scalby Primary School

Trust

I wish I could trust him,
I am giving him the responsibility -
Don't let me down!

I can trust you to free me,
Be honest, don't lie
I've got a lot of faith in you -
Betrayal is an insult to everyone
So tell the truth!

Don't be irresponsible and send me to jail.
He let me down.

Matthew Machin (10)
Newby & Scalby Primary School

Trust

I wish everyone was dependable.

My dog is my faithful friend.

I can rely on all my friends,

I am a loyal football fan,

I trust everyone to behave sensibly.

The players are devoted to the teams.

I am responsible for outdoor exercise.

Taylor Vasey (9)
Newby & Scalby Primary School

Trust

My friend is very untrustworthy,
I assume someone is my friend.
A fox is definitely unreliable.
Taylor is the most trustworthy person I know.
I have faith in my dad.
Matthew is a very reliable boy.
I accept we lost the hockey match.
I can convince my friends well.
Tiffany is very secretive,
I believe my friend can keep secrets.

Mathew Hume (10)
Newby & Scalby Primary School

Trust

My friend, I could rely on
To keep my secret, till he died.
He is loyal, honest and sincere.

I told him a secret
He kept it for a while
But one fatal day he told someone
I will never feel the same again.

Sam Simmons (9)
Newby & Scalby Primary School

Trust

My friend Mark is very reliable
He is also very loyal.
I can trust him with nearly anything,
I can share my secrets with him.
I have faith in my teammates
I can have a laugh with my pals
Betrayal, is an insult to everyone.

Luke Corden (10)
Newby & Scalby Primary School

Trust

Certain trust makes me feel calm,
I hope my family is trustworthy.
I trust my friends and family
I am reliable with my friends
I will tell the truth.

Your family is trustworthy forever,
They stand by you when you need help.

Trust is a responsibility
Trust is faith.

Ben Allen (10)
Newby & Scalby Primary School

My Little Brother

Aedan my brother, is naughty all the time,
(Oh no he isn't, I only said that to rhyme!)
But he pokes his finger into the hamster's cage,
When I tell him not to - he flies into a rage!
Sometimes when he's in a bad mood,
He simply will not eat his food.
He chases the cats until they can't run,
It seems to be his idea of fun!
He splashes in puddles - so he's covered in mud,
Then he splashes in the bath - until there seems to be a flood!
He takes the lid off the nappy cream,
The look upon his face is the cheekiest I've seen!
When he's laughing and smiling at me,
I know my brother's the best that he can be!

Dominique Evans (10)
Park Grove Primary School

Feelings

Together one day
Apart tomorrow,
Real life
Is much more sorrow.
I'll tell you what you have to do,
Don't be scared,
You'll pull through.
Another day,
Sun in the sky
Back together
No more cries.

Rachel Hampton   (10)
Park Grove Primary School

Mickey

Mickey is very dark and tall
He has his hair in the shape of a ball
Mickey wears 60's things
Such as flares and bracelets and rings

I think Mickey must be six foot three
As I only reach up to his knee
And that is quite odd, as I am ten
Mickey calls me his little hen!

But now I must leave you
It's time for bed
I need my sleep, there's a crazy day ahead!

Imogen Cole   (10)
Park Grove Primary School

Victoria

Victoria was a fat bloke
When she became queen
But when she was born
She was truly, very lean.

Victoria was eighteen
When she became queen
She was truly great
And sometimes, very mean.

'Go Victoria! Go Victoria!'
This is what people said
But poor people were scared of her
So they tucked up safe in bed.

Victoria was the greatest ruler
That England ever had
But people who hated her
Said that she was mad.

Albert was Victoria's husband
Very handsome, very tall, very lean
Although Victoria thought he was charming,
He was really quite mean.

Victoria's best friend
Was an old Scottish beard
He was a man named Mulley-Brown
That Mulley's name 's just weird.

Victoria had ministers
To help her with her work,
She didn't like Gladstone much
Because he always went beserk.

Victoria had nine children, one of them was a drunk
His name was Bertie and the people thought
He should be sunk!

Dipto Chowdhury (9)
Park Grove Primary School

Talent

Talent is all the colours of the rainbow
Glimmering and shimmering in the sunlight,
It smells like a newly picked rose,
From a garden of different flowers.
Talent tastes of sweet honey, freshly made
By bees that day.
It sounds like doves singing sweetly.
It feels like a soft cushion on a sofa,
Talent lives at the centre of your soul.

Bethan Davies (9)
Park Grove Primary School

Bath Time

Pitter-patter, pitter-patter (taps running)
Plong! Plank! Plong! Plank! (taps turning off)
Splish! Splash! Splosh! (jumping in the bath)
Woo! Woo! Woo! (putting bubble bath in)
Scrub a dub-dub (washing yourself)
Crash! Bang! Wallop! (getting out of the bath)
Brrrrrr! (drying yourself).

Jessica Dawson (9)
Park Grove Primary School

Snow

Snow is white, snow is soft
Snow is water turned into frost.
You can make snowballs and
Snowman too.
Snow feels like water poured onto your hand,
It looks like white icing on a cake.

Louis Dickinson (10)
Park Grove Primary School

Friendship

If it was a volcano
We seem to have erupted.
I'm feeling really
Really disrupted.

I don't understand
What is happening to me.
I don't understand
How I am meant to be.

I'm all out of friends,
All the ones I had
Said I'm going round the bend.
I'm feeling kind of sad.

Isobel Gordon   (9)
Park Grove Primary School

Teachers

I put a frog in his tea
Which made him poorly.
I tied little Freddie to a tree.
It makes the teacher
It makes the teacher
It makes the teacher *angry.*

I brought to school my pet flea
It dropped down the loo his car key.
It makes the teacher
It makes the teacher
It makes the teacher *angry.*

I put a sticker on his back saying 'kick me'
I put jelly in his welly.
It makes the teacher
It makes the teacher
It makes the teacher *angry.*

Jack Coverdale, Scott Bellamy & Chris Brelsford (11)
Riccall Primary School

Blue

Blue is the world above you,
Blue is the smell of bluebells,
Blue is the taste of berries,
Blue is the car that broke, down my street,
Blue is my bro's twinkling eyes, that I love,
Blue makes me shiver when
I watch the spooky movie,
Blue makes me smile,
Blue makes me feel cool
When I am fast asleep,
Blue is the water that I love the feel of,
Blue is the pair of jeans
That won't fit round my waist,
Blue is the water that comes
Out of the watering can,
Blue is the colour, cold,
Blue is the paper that was ripped,
Blue is my warm jumper,
I could not live without blue,
Could you?

Melissa Davies (8)
Riccall Primary School

Green

Green is the feeling of when I am ill,
Leaves floating down on the hill,
Plants growing up like a flash,
Crocodiles coming at you in a dash,
Green is grass; very spiky
And you go green when you feel jealous,
I could not live without green!
Could you?

Nadine Moore (8)
Riccall Primary School

Yeah And Boo!

'You can have some chewing gum.'
'Yeah!'
'After I've finished with it.'
'Boo!'
'We've got no more maths.'
'Yeah!'
'Because it's getting harder.'
'Boo!'
'We're getting playtime all day.'
'Yeah!'
'Because you have to stay in all week.'
'Boo!'

Hannah Mizen (7)
Riccall Primary School

Mum! Mum!

Mum! Mum! Why is Dad drinking rum!
Dad! Dad! You're making me sad!
Mum! Mum! This plum is yum!
Dad! Dad! That football is driving me mad!
Mum! Mum! My thumb feels numb!
Dad! Dad! My brother is being bad!
Mum! Mum! Tell Dad to stop that hum!
Dad! Dad! Can you add?
Mum! Mum! I can't do this sum.
Dad! Dad! Please make me glad.

Amy Dicks (7)
Riccall Primary School

I Have Never Seen . . .

I have never seen . . .
I have never seen . . .
A flying pig.

I have never seen . . .
I have never seen . . .
A wig doing a jig.

I have never seen . . .
I have never seen . . .
A talking book.

I have never seen . . .
I have never seen . . .
A floating book.

I have never seen . . .
I have never seen . . .
A clock wash its hands.

I have never seen . . .
I have never seen . . .
A fly play a band.

Isabelle LeMonnier (7)
Riccall Primary School

The Feel Of Things

I like the feel of my bed,
I like the feel of a thorn
But when I get it in my finger
I don't like it at all.
I like the feel of Dawn, my teddy,
When I go to sleep.
I like the feel of leather shoes,
I like the feel of my skin.
I even like the feel of when I grin.

Charlotte Horner (8)
Riccall Primary School

The Cool Mule

The mule, the mule who was born in Goole,
It was such a stupid fool,
Because it swallowed a sacred jewel,
While it was swimming in a pool.

The mule, the mule who was born in Goole.

Stole some fuel and a tool just to go blow up Riccall School,
Just as things couldn't get any worse,
He got in a duel with a hool
It was very cruel but he looked cool.

The mule, the mule who was born in Goole,
Used to rule and was very cool,
But now is a loner because it swallowed a jewel.

The mule, the mule . . .

Oh, what's the point?

Dean Frankish (11)
Riccall Primary School

It Makes My Teacher Mad!

Playing with their pens, click, click, click
Fighting in the playground, kick, kick, kick
Twanging rulers, ping, ping, ping
Choir out of tune, sing, sing, sing
Making lots of noise, chat, chat, chat
Playing on the PC, rat-a-tat-tat
Football through the window, smash, smash, smash
Noisy music lesson, crash, bash, crash
Children losing playtime, groan, groan, groan
Teachers in the staffroom, moan, moan, moan.

Andrew Beck & Karen Garbett (11)
Riccall Primary School

The Vampire

You have to admire,
The vampire, the vampire, the vampire
You have to admire the vampire, like a sapphire
Or else he'll turn you into fire, fire, fire
And call you a liar, a liar, a liar.

So you have to admire,
The vampire, the vampire, the vampire
You have to admire the vampire, like a sapphire.

He'd make you hire a wire, a wire, a wire
And you will walk on it till it expires, expires, expires.

So you have to admire,
The vampire, the vampire, the vampire
You have to admire the vampire, like a sapphire.

Alex Cogan (10)
Riccall Primary School

I've Never Seen . . .

I've never seen an elephant climb a tree,
Or a tiger shake hands with me,
Or a mouse swim in the sink,
Or the sky turn green and pink,
Or a wardrobe that could talk,
Or a bookcase that could walk,
Or a plant that had hair,
Or a dog eat an éclair,
Or a parrot eat a cake,
Or a monkey play with a grass snake,
Or a lion shave its fur,
Or a cat that doesn't purr.

Megan Young (9)
Riccall Primary School

You Can Have . . .

You can have my football . . . hooray!
It's flat . . . boo!

You can have my watch . . . hooray!
It has no battery . . . boo!

Arsenal 1 . . . hooray!
Chelsea 3 . . . boo!

You can have some sweets . . . hooray!
If you pay for them . . . boo!

You can have these crisps . . . hooray!
But they're out of date . . . boo!

You can have my mobile phone . . . hooray!
But there isn't a SIM card . . . boo!

You can have my ruler . . . hooray!
It's snapped . . . boo!

You can have my biscuit . . . hooray!
Wrapper . . . boo!

You can have my trampoline . . . hooray!
But it has a big hole in it . . . boo!

You can have a season ticket for United . . . hooray!
Leeds United . . . boo!

You can have my hamster . . . hooray!
But it's dead . . . boo!

You can have my pool table . . . hooray!
But there's no balls or cues . . . boo!

You can go in my swimming pool . . . hooray!
But there's no water . . . boo!

Sebastian Swain & Sam Elliott (11)
Riccall Primary School

You Can . . .

You can watch TV,
Hooray!
But you can't switch it on,
Boo!

You can buy some sweets,
Hooray!
But with your own money,
Boo!

Do you want some of my goldfish,
Hooray!
They're all dead,
Boo!

Do you want the last cookie,
Hooray!
I dropped it on the floor,
Boo!

It's your birthday son,
Hooray!
I've got you some socks,
Boo!

It's teatime,
Hooray!
How does cabbage stew sound?
Boo!

No school today,
Hooray!
They're coming to you instead,
Boo!

It's going to snow today,
Hooray!
But you're not going outside,
Boo!

Katie Falkingham & Kerry LeMonnier (11)
Riccall Primary School

Boo!

It's the weekend, *yeah!*
Got some homework, *boo!*

It's not much, *yeah!*
Write a poem, *boo!*

Nick Toczek came into our school, *yeah!*
Showed us how to write longer poems, *boo!*

He had brilliant ideas, *yeah!*
Now the teachers expect better poems, *boo!*

Nick performed magic, *yeah!*
Didn't explain how, *boo!*

We had a fantastic day, *yeah!*
But it was only a day, *boo!*

Bought one of his books, *yeah!*
Wait . . . I hate poetry, *boo!*

Finished this poem, *yeah!*
I like poetry now, *boo!*

Jack Hanslope (8)
Riccall Primary School

The Night I Heard A Bump

The night I heard a bump
My bed began to jump.
My heart began to flutter,
My belly felt like butter
I began to shout
But nothing came out
I began to mutter
But could not utter

   . . . *a sound!*

Samuel Seabrooke (8)
Riccall Primary School

The Day I Drove My Mum Up The Wall

I'm going to mess up my room,
Because it drives my mum up the wall.

I'm going to make a loud noise like boom,
Because it drives my mum up the wall.

I'm not going to wash the pots,
Because it drives my mum up the wall.

I'm going to eat my Jelly Tots,
Because it drives,
Because it drives,
Because it drives my mum up the wall.

I'm not going to be a fool,
Because it drives my mum up the wall.

I'm going to nick her jewel,
Because it drives my mum up the wall.

I'm going to act like a bat,
Because it drives my mum up the wall.

I'm going to tell her she's fat,
Because it drives,
Because it drives,
Because it drives my mum up the wall!

Alice Smith (10)
Riccall Primary School

Monsters In The Dark

Things that go bump in the night. Leaves rustling.
Trains going by or maybe a monster at your bedside!

The monster is hairy and grizzly inside
And most of his hairs could touch both his eyes!

His toes are triangular and his face is a square
His feet are as big as a circle - *beware!*

Amy Parish (7)
Riccall Primary School

I've Never Seen . . .

I've never seen . . .
A newspaper race
Or a book wash its face.

I've never seen . . .
A mountain with hands
Or a horse throw a band.

I've never seen . . .
A Christmas tree dance
Or a bean get in a trance.

I've never seen . . .
A coconut cook
Or a stupid talking book.

I've never seen . . .
A car drink
Or a bush wink.

I've never seen . . .
A monkey fly.

Paul Winterburn (9)
Riccall Primary School

A Summer Poem

Butterflies fluttering,
Baby birds scuttering,
Bumblebees busy,
Children so dizzy.
Horses canter and prance
Leaves sway and dance
Sun burning hot
We eat ice cream a lot.
Pretty flower in full bloom
And I've still got to tidy my room.

Fiona Berry (9)
Riccall Primary School

My Baby Brother

Ten little fingers,
Ten little toes,
Two blue eyes
And one button nose.

One big grin,
Two pixie ears,
Always crying,
Piercing tears.

Ten little fingers,
Ten little toes,
Two blue eyes
And one button nose.

Three smelly nappies,
In the bin,
Heinz baby food
In a tin.

Ten little fingers,
Ten little toes,
Two blue eyes
And one button nose.

He closes his eyes,
Shh, be quiet,
He peacefully lies!

Karen Garbett & Hayley Scott (11)
Riccall Primary School

My Dad

My dad is as strong as a knight
He's the best and really bright.
He loves his noisy chainsaw
But loves woodwork even more
He's the best as you can see
I love him and he loves me.

Ellie Watts (9)
Riccall Primary School

The Vampire's Underwear

In the middle of the night,
An ugly vampire gave me a fright.
He really gave me a scare,
Dancing in his underwear.

> Dancing in his,
> Dancing in his,
> Underwear.

He then grabbed my left wrist tight,
And lunged in for a bite.
But he missed me and hit air,
Dancing in his underwear.

> Dancing in his,
> Dancing in his,
> Underwear.

He missed to my delight,
And I was quite alright.
But the vampire didn't care,
Dancing in his underwear.

> Dancing in his,
> Dancing in his,
> Underwear.

In the middle of the night,
An ugly vampire gave me a fright.
He really gave me a scare,
Dancing in his underwear.

Helen Winterburn (11)
Riccall Primary School

The Sock Man

There was an old man called Fred
Who liked to eat hard bread,
He went around
Making a sound
And wore a sock on his head.

Charlie Swain (9)
Riccall Primary School

Makes Dad Mad!

Look I've found some slugs,
I've seen some frogs' spawn!
I'll mix them both together,
And spread it on the lawn!

Because it makes Dad,
Makes my dad,
Makes my dad mad!

I'm gonna run upstairs,
And trash up all his room!
Then I'll see how he likes it,
Crash! Bang! Boom!

Because it makes Dad,
Makes my dad,
Makes Dad mad!

If you look under my bed,
There's a can of paint!
I'm gonna splodge it on the wall
And make my dad faint!

Because it makes Dad,
Makes my dad,
Makes Dad mad!

I'm gonna run outside,
And get my ball so . . .
That when I kick it really hard,
It'll smash the window!

Because it makes Dad,
Makes my dad,
And everybody mad!

Alice Pomfret (9)
Riccall Primary School

The Evil Ghoul

He was born in a pool
He nicked off with a jewel
He hid in a school
He got out his tool
And he started to duel
They called him a fool
He was really cruel
He was a terrifying ghoul
He'll be in jail till Yule
He exploded the school
He fell over a stool
And got kicked by a mule
Then he rescued a jewel from the school.

Nathan Wilson (9)
Riccall Primary School

Fairy Dust

When fairy dust twirls,
It shines like red pearls,
Reaching for the sky,
Sometimes lands in apple pie.

When fairy dust twinkles
It gets rid of wrinkles,
Really when it twinkles people like Pringles,
It really is magical.

Sarah Owen (6)
Riccall Primary School

A Vampire

A vampire in the night
With a vicious bite, bite, bite
Ooh, what a fright
A vampire in the night
With sharp teeth of white, white, white
Ooh, what a fright
A vampire in the night.

A vampire in the night
Better not get in a fight, fight, fight
Ooh, what a fright a vampire in the night
Spreading his cape like a kite, kite, kite
Ooh, what a fright
A vampire in the night.

He soars into the sky at midnight, midnight
Ooh, what a fright
A vampire in the night
A vampire
A vampire
A vampire in the night.

Sarah Larkin & Rachel Olipant (11)
Riccall Primary School

The Dragon's Snack

Help, help, a dragon has swallowed my mum.
I can see her wriggling in his tum.
Spit her out, she's no snack,
She's my mum so give her back,
I'll get my dad, he's big and bad
He'll get my mum from the dragon's tum,
When she gets out you better run
Because she'll put you in a bun
And eat you for her tea.

Finn Northrop (6)
Riccall Primary School

Thing

A world of eternity
A world of continuity
A world without light.
Cave man
Pitch-black
As he rubs two sticks together
Suddenly
Thing roars into life
A flickering plume
Of golden-yellow
Dies down
Red . . . blue . . . black
Now a grey pile of ash
An irreversible change.
Seven thousand years later
Science lesson
Children bored
They've seen it all before
Teacher strikes match . . .
Oooohhhhh!
Children still struck
By magical beauty
And wonder of *thing*
A world of eternity
A world of continuity
A world without light.

Kathryn Butterworth (11)
St Mary's CE Primary School, York

Fire

F ire is a tiger roaring with rage darting about all over the place.
I t is burning its prey to death.
R oaring and snarling for more food.
E ating through the flesh of its prey.

Jack Bradford (10)
St Mary's CE Primary School, York

In The Night

Silent as a mouse
But as deadly as a lion
The smoke creeps under your door
In the night
You're sleeping peacefully in your bed,
Little do you know that
You're in danger
In the night, in the night
The fire bell is blaring
You hear the crackle,
But no way out
You are trapped
In the night, in the night
You cough as the smoke chokes you
As the flames beat down your door
And you are dying
In the night, in the night.

Alan Drever-Smith (11)
St Mary's CE Primary School, York

Fire

Fire, fire everywhere,
Do we go near it?
No we don't dare.
Where it goes
No one knows.
It's orange and red, burning hot.
The smoke can kill with one deadly shot,
It's just like gold silk, flowing through the air,
Then gone.
Never to be seen again,
All that is left is ash and pain.

Charlie Robson (11)
St Mary's CE Primary School, York

The Sea

The sea can be a kitten lapping its way up the golden soft sand.
It can change in a moment to a dangerous lion,
Up-turning ships and beaching whales.

Colours change, aqua, blue and varying shades of grey
Aqua, shallow and warm beckoning us to paddle.
Blue, deep and calm, how about a swim?
Grey, cold and angry. Stay clear, don't come in!

Chris Archer (11)
St Mary's CE Primary School, York

Fire Is A Killer

Fire is a killer. It burns. It kills.
The smoky scent floating in the air
Damaging people's lives.
The ashes lying on the floor.
People rushing in and a child lying there.
Silent. Dead.
Fire is a killer. It burns. It kills.

Tamsin Boynton (10)
St Mary's CE Primary School, York

The Fire

Floats along its prey
Thought to be gone,
Instead, comes back with a pounce
Just to remind you where he has been
He leaves a scent, the deadly killer
When the beast has done the damage
He stalks away.

Jessica Gillam (11)
St Mary's CE Primary School, York

Fire

Fire sad, fire angry, fire scared, fire happy.
Fire red, yellow, blue and orange.
Fire is a rainbow tall and strong.
Fire fierce, fire frightened, fire fragile, fire carries on.

Sophie Wain-Williams (10)
St Mary's CE Primary School, York

A Fire

A fire, it's mean, kills people it sees,
A fire, it smells of smoking, burning trees,
A fire goes crackle and hiss in the night,
Smoke seeping through and under a door
Giving you such a fright!

Matthew Myers (11)
St Mary's CE Primary School, York

Fire

F ire is a raging killer.
I t attacks all it meets.
R evenge is what it seeks.
E verything it joins to stands no chance.

Lauren Dodd (11)
St Mary's CE Primary School, York

Fire

F ire is a blue, orange flame
I t is a big giant coming to get you
R arr! It goes as you dart off trying to get away.
E asily get its power at you as it smokes away.

Hannah Bartram (9)
St Mary's CE Primary School, York

Fire

The match crunches as it strikes,
The flame goes wild as it is brought
To the candle and paper.
The flame nibbles at the candle,
Feasts on the paper.
The colours change and change,
Yellow to orange,
Orange to red,
Sometimes blue!
The wax melts, the paper burns,
The candle is no more,
The paper has blacked.
You pick up the paper,
Warm
Crumbly
Soft
Soft
Soft ash.

Rachel Neylon (10)
St Mary's CE Primary School, York

Fire Tornado

Our class went to Magna on Tuesday.
We saw a fire tornado.
I saw a fire sizzling, silent smoke rising,
I saw the yellow and orange flames.
The swirling fire tornado,
I smell smoke slithering along like a snake,
Crackling sparks of red then it stops.
Then, just 10 minutes later,
It starts up again, swirling with pretty patterns,
I feel the heat against my face.

Chloe Smith (9)
St Mary's CE Primary School, York

Smoke

Forked,
Once was fizzing,
Frightfully
In fire.
Chalky,
Choking,
Away with the bright
Orange of flame
Passed,
Around the class
In a bubble of fear.
Faces are glumming
People,
Running.
The death ring,
Of the siren
Overpowering.

Jake Millson (11)
St Mary's CE Primary School, York

Fire: Beware

Fire burns.
Blue, yellow and orange fill your eyes.
The hungry beast is feeding.
Smoke fills the room. A killer.
The heat warms you up.
You hear ambulances and fire engines.
You finally see them.
Water is sprayed.
Flash, the fire goes out.
Ash is spilt everywhere.
Someone, lying on the floor, *dead.*

Abigail Mastin (9)
St Mary's CE Primary School, York

What Is Fire?

Fire is a lion,
It roars menacingly
Then pounces proudly on its prey
Providing a spectacular display of crimson, gold and yellow.
Once finished with the dead it slyly searches for its next victim.

Fire is a dragon
With a mane of pure embers
That delights yet destroys China.
Cong Hi Fa Choi, it is not
People run from the noble flames
As it illuminates the sky and in turn the dusky streets.

Fire is an evil spirit
It lives within the core of the blaze
As it stealthily creeps into the air
And wavers out to reveal the spectral delight
Of the evanescent colours.
Glimmering shades of orange and maroon
The fire connects with the lost souls.
Reignited and reincarnated.

Fire - a fabulous fiend.

Abbie Girling (11)
St Mary's CE Primary School, York

Killer

F ire is a deadly weapon,
I mmortal flame,
R eveals all anger in destruction,
E very time it could claim its next victim!

Andrew Myers (11)
St Mary's CE Primary School, York

Fire! Fire!

Fire is bright,
bright and hot.
Fire flickers, flashes
in the moonlight.
Fire changes,
transforms colour.
Fire smells, smells
like a barbecue.

Megan Skelton (10)
St Mary's CE Primary School, York

Fire

Crackle, burn, you hear it say.
Angry, burning against your eyes.
Orange, blue, its colour changes.
White paper, brown paper.
Dry, warm ashes, soft, cold ashes.
Changing by seconds
Through burning its soft self.

Imogen Toulmin (10)
St Mary's CE Primary School, York

Fire Poem

F ire is fierce, fierce and angry.
I mages change every time it burns,
   first yellow then orange and finally blue.
R eally hot, really warm even when the ashes are torn.
E asily crumbles, easily crisps,
   smells very strong and very smoky.

Jessica Wray (11)
St Mary's CE Primary School, York

The School Bully

One day I was walking to school,
I bumped into the school bully.
He said, 'My name is Billy -
I'm going to bully you at school,
See you at school, Tinkerbell.'
When Tinkerbell and Billy were face to face
The teacher saw Tinkerbell shivering and worried
The teacher sent Billy home
He never bullied anyone ever again.

Ashleigh Arnold (7)
Spennithorne CE Primary School

The Busy Builder

I saw a busy builder
Building with some bricks,
I asked him what his name was
And he said, 'Mr Hicks.'

I asked what he was building,
He said, 'A garden shed,'
'How long are you building for?'
'Until it's time for bed!'

Daisy Roe (7)
Spennithorne CE Primary School

The Baboon

On my way to school I saw a baboon.
It was a hairy baboon,
It was a big hairy baboon,
It was an ugly, big hairy baboon,
It was a stinky, ugly, big hairy baboon,
It was a dumb, stinky, ugly, big hairy baboon,
And it was coming to get me!

Jeremy J Foster (7)
Spennithorne CE Primary School

The Moose

On my way to school I saw a moose.
It was a hairy moose,
It was an ugly, hairy moose,
It was an enormous, ugly, hairy moose,
It was a bouncing, enormous, ugly, hairy moose,
It was a spotty, bouncing, enormous, ugly, hairy moose,
And it wanted to squash me!

Ellie Cooke (8)
Spennithorne CE Primary School

The Crocodile

On my way to school
I saw a crocodile.
It was a green crocodile,
It was a shiny green crocodile,
It was a fat, shiny green crocodile,
It was an old, fat, shiny green crocodile,
It was a little, old, fat, shiny green crocodile
And it wanted to eat me!

Will Stephenson (7)
Spennithorne CE Primary School

Sadness Is . . .

A pizza without spicy sausage,
grey,
a rainy day,
a hungry lion.

Lloyd Plews (6)
Spennithorne CE Primary School

Scary Poem

Once when I was asleep I heard
Something scratching on my floor.
I woke up and put my light on,
I looked around
But there was nothing there.
I felt very scared,
I was going to go back into my bedroom
But I felt too scared
So I went to Mummy's
And it was pitch-black
When I got there
I quietly stepped in to Mummy's and Daddy's bedroom
Then I woke Mummy up
And Daddy up.
Daddy got up and checked my bedroom
But there was nothing there.
In the morning Mummy found who it was . . .
It was my kitten, Poppy.

Sophie Walton (7)
Spennithorne CE Primary School

Wolf In The Midnight

One midnight I woke up
And looked around.
Suddenly I saw
A shadow of a wolf.
Bravely I ran to my mummy's bedroom
And snuggled up.

Then I heard scratching
All around me.

Emily Milverton (7)
Spennithorne CE Primary School

The Creepy Tree

It was a cold, misty night,
All was quiet, it was blackness outside,
Everyone in the house was asleep except for me.
There was a noise -
A tree tapping on my window,
My hair on end
Every time it tapped.
I kept in to the beat,
It was tap tap tap,
I opened my bedroom window and pushed
The tree away.
It still kept tapping,
But got louder and louder.
I ran in my mum's room,
'There is a tree tapping,
On my window.'
'I will come and have a look.'
'It is annoying, it should stop.'
'I can still hear it.'
'Just go to sleep,
Just shut up!'

Kate Kitchingman (7)
Spennithorne CE Primary School

Dracula

It was one starry night
When the wind was howling strangely.
I saw a figure down the hall.
My hair stood on end,
His eyes were red.
His fangs dripping with blood.
It was . . .

Dracula!

Callum Carlisle (7)
Spennithorne CE Primary School

Danny The Bully

I was walking to school when I saw Danny.
He said, 'I'm going to beat you up.'
I just ignored him
And knew not to worry.
I tried not to put a worried look on my face.
I went to the school gates
I forgot all about him.
It soon was hometime.
At 2 o'clock I said bye to Wilma and my friends,
I went walking home.
I went to my room.
I played with my brother Timmy.

Amy Leathley (7)
Spennithorne CE Primary School

School Bully

One day I was walking to school
And Merton grabbed me from behind
And pushed me over.
I ran to school as fast as I could.
When I got to school
I told the headteacher all about it.
The headteacher was very surprised.
When Merton got to school
He got the whip out
Of the box.

Georgina Laws (7)
Spennithorne CE Primary School

School Bully

On my way to school
I saw a boy who came out of his gateway.
He was called Dick.
He called me a nasty name.
I felt unhappy but I soon forgot about it
When I saw my friend.
I went on my way
To school with my friends.
I told the teacher
And the bully went to
The top of the stairs.

Emily Jefferson (7)
Spennithorne CE Primary School

If I Was On The Moon

If I was on the moon
I would run and shout,
Eating all the cheese
That was lying about.

After I'd finished,
And I'd eaten it all,
I'd look down on Earth
And cry, 'Isn't it small?'

When it got late
I would ask the moon,
'When will I see you again?'
And the moon would answer,
'Very soon.'

Jennifer Anderson (9)
Stockton-on-the-Forest CP School

The Moon

The moon shines like a glimmering eyeball
And looks at you in the dark,
So watch out.

The moon shines like a white limousine
With people coming out.

The moon shines like a fresh rubber
About to be used.

The moon shines like a caravan
Glooming in the darkness.

The moon shines like a new
Fresh piece of paper.

The moon shines like a
New stereo being bought.

The moon shines like a bald man
With no hair.

The moon shines like a
New white book.

The moon shines like a PlayStation
Here comes the moon's friend.

Luke Howden (8)
Stockton-on-the-Forest CP School

Senses

I like to smell my mum's home-made rock buns
I like to hear my mum shouting me for tea.
I like to touch my rabbit's fur when it is wet.
I like to feel my rabbit's fur when it is wet.
I like to taste lots of sweets when they are in my mouth. Yum!

Maya Blakeway (8)
Stockton-on-the-Forest CP School

The Moon

The moon shines like cats' eyes
The moon is like a ball of wool
The moon is as white as a sheep
If I was on the moon I would eat all the cheese
Until I was too fat.

The moon helps me to see in the dark
The moon is a surfer that lights up the sky
The moon sparkles like a diamond
The moon's as white as my teeth
The moon shines like headlights.

The moon shivers like a diamond in the sky
There comes the shine of the sun
And so the moon goes away.

Liam Coughlin (8)
Stockton-on-the-Forest CP School

Senses

I like the smell of my nan's home-made pies.
I like the smell of petrol.
When I go to see my dad the smell of pizza cooking.

I like the touch of my skin and my cold bed cover at night.
My silk pyjamas in my drawer folded up.

I love the taste of chocolate when it's sweetie night
And the taste of toffee apples on Bonfire Night.

I love the sound of rain on the windowpane.
My friends on the phone and pencils snapping.

I like to see my friends at school,
My hamster's cage at night and the sunset.

Samantha Fraser (9)
Stockton-on-the-Forest CP School

The Moon

The moon looks like a cheeky face.
The moon looks like a big, nice, juicy eye that stares at us.
A bumpy cheese hopped out, well that's what we thought it was
And it was really a funny-shaped moon.

The moon looks like white chocolate ready to eat.
The moon gleams like a star in the dark seas.
The moon looks like cotton wool and snow.

If I was on the moon I would sit there all day and imagine
And would eat with Martians around the moon
Eating the cheese like me.

One nice, sunny and bright day it's nice and fun
And soon it gets loud, shivery, dark and scary
And the people screamed, where am I. Soon they will be asleep
Then the moon sneaks and creeps up for a good night's sleep.

The moon shines while the stars twinkle at night
When the sun goes down into someone's mouth.
The moon is bright like a new light bulb,

And here comes the sun covering the moon away
And making it all bright.

Daniel Langford (7)
Stockton-on-the-Forest CP School

The Stars

The stars shine like
lots of diamonds in a treasure chest.
The stars shine like
white buttons floating on a black blanket.
The stars shine like
a pearl in an oyster's mouth.
When the stars disappear,
the sun comes up.

Jamie Richardson (8)
Stockton-on-the-Forest CP School

The Moon

The moon shines like a diamond in the sky and a cat's eye.
The moon shines like a white world in the sea.
It looks like a lump of cheese
And a white balloon that makes you sleep.

The moon has its own story and it looks like a white sun.
It is like a big ball of wool.

The moon looks like a ball of snow melting
As it moves further and further away.
It is a beautiful sight for you and me.
It is as pretty as a light yet still shimmering.

The moon shines like a star on a tree with a lump of snow on top.
Only if I could speak to it I would ask, what is your story
I would like to know. Just if I could speak it to you.

Danielle Bell (9)
Stockton-on-the-Forest CP School

Senses Poem

I like the smell of steak.
I like the smell of nicely cooked bacon.
I like the smell of ribs.
I like the smell of petrol.

I like to watch TV.
I like to watch the cars zooming past.
I like watching my cat.
I like to watch the busy people outside.
I like to eat sweets.

I like to feed my cat at night.
I like to watch the shooting stars in summer.

Jordan Fletcher (7)
Stockton-on-the-Forest CP School

The Moon

The moon shines like a football out of its box,
Shimmering like a gold diamond.
It's stupid as a clown, it's like a sphere.
It's as white as a mouse.

It's as steamy as a fire.
The moon is like a jellyfish in the air.
It's as angry as a monster,
It's as scary as a roller coaster
And as strange as an eagle.

Teeth as sharp as a cheetah's
And as pale as a person.
Its mouth is like a round circle.
It's as furry as a cat.
It looks like cotton wool,
It's also like a hot air balloon.

Tommy Hields (7)
Stockton-on-the-Forest CP School

The Stars

The stars shine like big pieces of foil
In a dark, royal treasure chest.

The stars gleam like shimmering star jewels
As clean as a new silver ring.

The stars shimmer like a bag of gold
Buried in a hole stolen from the sun.

The stars float over a dark cloak
Like a fish on top of the sea.

The stars shiver like crowns flying down
From the sky in darkness,
No more stars as the sun returns.

Cassie Hields (8)
Stockton-on-the-Forest CP School

The Moon

The moon shines like a shimmering diamond,
Lonely in a blanket of stars.
The moon shines like cats' eyes.
The moon looks like a ball of wool.

The moon shines like sheep's wool.
A diamond in a treasure chest of stars,
A jewel sparkling in blackness.

Here comes the sun
And says good morning to the moon.

Abbie Seavers (8)
Stockton-on-the-Forest CP School

Senses

I love to smell roses and my hamster
When she has just been cleaned out.

I love to touch my hamster's fur
And to touch hard and soft wood.

I love to taste sweets and chocolate
And apple because they taste nice.

I like to listen to cars whizzing by.

I love to see bees going into flowers.

Bethany Raine (8)
Stockton-on-the-Forest CP School

The Moon

The moon is like a massive diamond in the sky.
The moon shines like white gold sparkling in the dark.
The moon is like a silver disco ball shimmering in the darkness.
The moon shines and gleams and shivers
Floating along the sky until the sun comes.

Nathan Bargate (8)
Stockton-on-the-Forest CP School

Stars

Stars gleam in my eyes like car headlights,
lots of diamonds shimmering on the dark blanket of night.

They're like bits of shattered pencil lead
scattered on a newly painted table,
new shiny hub caps on a flashy sports car.

Stars are like bits of torn up tinfoil,
like smooth bits of candyfloss on sticks.

Stars are kidnapped by the sun's light.

Katherine Wilson (8)
Stockton-on-the-Forest CP School

The Moon

The moon shines like a star sparkling in space.
The moon is a shape of a clock on a table.

The moon is the colour of a cloud floating in the sky.
The moon is like my head shimmering in space.

The moon is the colour of a cloud.
The moon is as bright as a light.

Charlie Kirkpatrick (7)
Stockton-on-the-Forest CP School

Senses

I like to taste my mum's milkshake in the sun.
I like to smell banana in my milkshake.
I like to touch jelly when it has come out of the fridge.
I like to hear the sound of the TV in the background at bedtime.
I like to see my favourite programme on the TV.

Hannah Hall (8)
Stockton-on-the-Forest CP School

The Moon

If I was on the moon, I would drink all of the milk
When I had finished drinking,
The moon would feel like soft, smooth milk.
The moon is shaped like a gigantic sofa in the black ocean.
It looks like mashed sugar in the shimmering darkness.
The moon is like a ball of wool ready for a kitten to play with.
Too lunar its wall are like an enormous ice cream.
It shimmers like a queen's crown
Ready for her to sit on her throne.
Here comes the moon's best friend, the sun.
It hides then as it shines brightly.

Jade Temperton (8)
Stockton-on-the-Forest CP School

The Moon

Sparkling diamond in the sky.
Lies in the air.
Smiles while out at night.

Big lump of cheese ready to squeeze and eat.
Sitting there in the dark.

Children looking out of their windows at bedtime,
Wondering if it's slime.
Then the next day's rays surprise the moon.

Bye-bye moon!

Emma Hamilton (9)
Stockton-on-the-Forest CP School

The Moon

The moon shines like a diamond, a diamond that never fades.
The moon looks like it has been covered in milk
And it looks like an eye that looks at you when you're asleep.

If I was the moon I would bounce and cry with joy,
I would eat all the cheese that surrounded me.

If I was to look down on Earth I would say that it is small.

The moon shines through the night,
It doesn't half give you a fright!

Whilst the moon is on holiday in LA,
The sun guides us through the day.

Emma Whitson (8)
Stockton-on-the-Forest CP School

Sea Angel

I scooped up a beautiful seashell
And gently put it against my ear,
All the clashing sounds were placed in my head,
The sea crashed on the sandy beach,
Dolphins sprung into the air,
Fish leapt gracefully out of the salty sea,
Sharks dived eagerly down deep into the sea,
Seaweed calmly floated around the surface of the sea.

Emma Leeming (8)
Thornton-in-Craven Community Primary School

Seashell

I put the seashell to my ear
and heard a tail swishing in the water
and dolphins diving high above
while a crab was nibbling soft seaweed.

Alex Pilling (8)
Thornton-in-Craven Community Primary School

Sea Life

As I lift the old battered shell to my ear,
I listen to the sea's fantasies about . . .

Ten-foot manta rays swooping past coral,
The angry sea smashing against rocks,
The swishing tails of sharks and dolphins,
The silver pearls glinting,
The whale yawning,
The mermaids talking,
This is what I hear,
When I lift the shell to my ear.

Callum Higgins (8)
Thornton-in-Craven Community Primary School

Sea Star

I picked up a shell
And I hear all the ocean.
Sounds of waves
Whooshing and crashing on the beach.
I hear the shark's teeth clashing
And whales making underwater sounds.
As the sea calms down
And the waves stop crashing
Rippling waves go tiptoeing into caves.

Emily Teall (7)
Thornton-in-Craven Community Primary School

Sea Life

Put a shell to your ear,
Hear the fishes swish their tails,
I hear the plants shiver,
Listen to the sea twirl,
I listen to the rock crumble against the surface.

Alex Walker (7)
Thornton-in-Craven Community Primary School

The Cockle Shell

As I lift it to my ear
The gleaming wave-washed shell,
I can hear;
Shining pearls floating through the sea,
Rays shoot through,
The small underwater tunnels,
Splash! A cannonball hits the sand,
Plants die,
Fish dive,
And suddenly
The sea is normal,
Everything is normal.

Alex Sharrad (9)
Thornton-in-Craven Community Primary School

Sea

I pick up a shell
And I put it to my ear
Different sounds come into my head.
I can hear the gentle sound of the sea
Whooshing onto the beach.
The seaweed shivered side to side
While the sea chants.
I can also hear the splashing sound
Of the whale's tail
As the dolphins leap through the air.

Milly Gates (9)
Thornton-in-Craven Community Primary School

Under The Sea

When I lift a seashell to my ear
This is what I hear;
Manta rays hover in the sea
Just like birds flying through the sky,
Horse fish suck on seaweed
Like a horse chomping on grass,
Penguins on the surface
Like an eagle high above the rest,
Whales swimming together
Like giant trucks in a hurry,
Clownfish making other fish swim away
Like the worst clown in the world!

Dale Terry (9)
Thornton-in-Craven Community Primary School

Sea Sounds

I pick up the shell,
And I put it in my ear,
I hear waves shouting,
Sharks jumping side to side,
Whales talking to me,
Stingrays moving stealthily.
The sea sounds like a wolf,
The sea looks like a big dog,
I hear crabs nipping seaweed,
Dolphins jumping head over heels,
You hear powerful wind,
And beach balls bouncing.

James Nicholas (8)
Thornton-in-Craven Community Primary School

Magical Shells

Lift a gleaming shell to your ear,
Hear the lashing sea in your head.

Hear the whooshing great white shark splashing.
Discover the buzz of the jellyfish.
Absorb the crill scampering away.
Listen to the big blue whale yawning in the sea.
Dolphins splashing up and down.
Crabs nipping at a little piece of seaweed.
Listen to sea clams bubbling in the sea.

Sidney Shorten (8)
Thornton-in-Craven Community Primary School

Sea Poem

The sea is equipped with enemies and anemones.
The swooping sounds of the wind hitting the water.

I can hear the rustling of the seaweed.
I can hear the snapping of the crabs.

In the shell I can hear the feet of the children creeping away.
Splash! Go the dolphins.
Scuttling of the water insects.
The children have really gone.

Stanley Bowley (9)
Thornton-in-Craven Community Primary School

The Wonderful Seashell

I put the shell to my ear,
And I heard some wonderful sounds.
I heard the whooshing sound of a stingray,
And I heard the sound of whale's
Warble, with water coming out of it,
And I heard the flapping tail of a clownfish.

Sam Mavor (7)
Thornton-in-Craven Community Primary School

The Sea

As I lift the shell to my ear,
Different sounds I hear.
The sea wriggles on the sand,
The coral waves in the breeze,
Fish are swimming round,
It is like a turtle walking,
The water rushes away,
Everything is quiet, still,
Everything is still,
The waves have washed away,
The sea goes normal.

Michael Stoker (8)
Thornton-in-Craven Community Primary School

What Is . . .

What is the sun?
The sun is a huge embarrassed face.

Where does the sky begin?
Over the hills and round the bushes.

Where does time go?
Into a giant clock in the centre of the Earth.

What is inside a hill?
Gigantic strawberry sweets.

Is life a dream?
Life is a wonderful dream with great things.

How do windows see?
Through their top two eyes.

What is inside a waterfall?
A giant pot of gold.

How does wind speak?
With a loud moan and a groan.

Jared Longhorne (11)
Thorpe Willoughby CP School

The Sound Collector

(Based on 'The Sound Collector' by Roger McGough)

'A stranger called this morning
Dressed all in black and grey
Put every sound into a bag
And carried it away'

The noise of panting children
The scratching of the pens
The zipping-up of pencil cases
The children counting up in tens

The humming of the yellow lights
The creaking of the heavy door
The loud noise of teachers
The gnawing of the metal saw

The dropping of the stripy pencils
The scraping of the chair
The ticking of the clock
The hurt children in care

The bouncing of the balls outside
The rustling of the papers
The clicking of the keyboard
The naughty upset escapers

The swishing of the blinds
The teachers as they shout 'vite'
The flicking of the pages
The cleaners humming as
They sweep

'A stranger called this morning
He didn't leave his name
Left us only silence
Life will never be the same.'

Eleanor Craven (11)
Thorpe Willoughby CP School

Snowman

Today it is snowing
and the wind is blowing
the kids are cheering
to see snowmen appearing

Children are happy
so let's get snappy
to have a snow fight
before it becomes night.

James Thomas (8)
Thorpe Willoughby CP School

My Angel

Angels are special things.
They all have big, beautiful wings.
They fly around without a sound,
But never can be found, but when the
Sun shines I know my angel's around.
She makes my heart and soul go round.
She's my angel, she's my soul, she's my
Sister, laughing up in Heaven.

Leah Mathias (9)
Thorpe Willoughby CP School

My Best Buddy!

Emily's my best buddy,
She loves to study,
But her hair's a mess,
She couldn't care less.

Emma Jennison (8)
Thorpe Willoughby CP School

What Is?

What is the sun?
A huge sunflower.

Where does the sky begin?
Where the Earth ends and over the hills.

Where does time go?
Time gets sucked into your watch.

What is inside a hill?
A witch's cave.

Is life a dream?
Everyone's life is a dream.

How does a window see?
Through the corner of its eyes.

What is inside a waterfall?
A life of dreams beyond your head.

How does the wind speak?
By whispering to us.

Ailsa Stainthorpe (10)
Thorpe Willoughby CP School

Hot And Cold

Hot is red
Hot is scary
Hot makes my fingers tingle
Hot is red

Cold is blue
Cold is nasty
It feels like sinking
Cold makes the wind blow
Cold is blue.

Emma Gough (8)
Thorpe Willoughby CP School

The Mad Monster

He sleeps at day
He wakes at night
He creeps about
With such delight
And when you go into your room
You've signed a contract for your doom
So go into your room real slow
If you're lucky he won't know
So when you wake up in the night
Don't blame me, you've had a fright
Can't you see?
He's a hairy fairy
A muddy buddy
A fuddy duddy
He only wants a friend
He'll keep up all the mischief
Right until the end.

Rebecca Coupland (10)
Thorpe Willoughby CP School

Children

Children are nice
but sometimes get lice

Children have brains
and love to play games

Children have fun
and they love to run

If they go too fast
they fall on their bum!

Sophie Billingsley (8)
Thorpe Willoughby CP School

All Sorts Of Weather

The dark night,
The warmth mild,
The lightning bright,
The storm wild.

Fences rattling,
Thunder growling,
Flowerpots shattering,
Wind howling.

Then the lightning stops,
The wind has stopped growing,
Still shattered are the flowerpots,
But the wind quietly still blowing.

Silent goes the thunder,
Silent goes the lightning,
But then I start to wonder,
Where is the brightening,
Of the lightning.

Then the sun comes out,
And the day gets bright,
Now I can go out and about,
The lightning is not there to fright.

Now the storm has gone,
But there are still some big puddles,
Now it is just the sun,
But I can still play in puddles.

But then I felt a chill on my nose,
Then I saw a little snowflake fall,
Then some snowfall that glows
I thought, *soon I might be able to*
Make some snowballs.

I dashed inside to tell my mum,
And my daddy too,
'There's no more sun today,
Instead there is some snow.'

Later that day I went outside,
To see how much snow,
All the puddles had turned into ice,
Then I felt a chill again on my nose,
And my toes began to tingle in a way that's nice.

Next I built a snowman,
A really big one too,
In this weather you surely can't get a suntan,
But I am glad I played in the snow.

Then the snow stops falling,
But I don't go inside,
I carry on snowballing,
But if only I could go for a skiing ride.

Then the snow starts to melt,
But then I felt a stone fall on my head,
And then the hailstones start to pelt,
There is no more snow, just hail instead.

Melissa Nix (9)
Thorpe Willoughby CP School

Shadow

In the moonlight what
Can you see?
What could it be?
What could it be?
Could it be a cat
Sat on a tree?
What could it be?
Have a closer look
Then you'll see, it's only me.

Emily Jackson (8)
Thorpe Willoughby CP School

Children

Children are nice
They sometimes have fights
Best friends are cosy
One is called Sophie.

Friends can be girls
With hair that has curls
Some children are small
But some are quite tall.

Friends can be boys
That play with good toys
Game Boys are cool
But sometimes they're fools.

Robert Chadwick (8)
Thorpe Willoughby CP School

Weather I Like

When we have snow,
We wrap so warm we start to glow.

When we have sleet,
We use the fire to keep in the heat.

When we have rain,
It splashes and dashes on my windowpane.

When we have sun,
We go to the park and have lots of fun.

Splitter, splatter on the door,
That's the snow that came before.

Marcus Loveday (9)
Thorpe Willoughby CP School

The Witch's Spell

Spin, spin with a spoon
Let a fire roar up to the moon

A shiny slug, a misty fly
A full mug, a pirate's eye
An ugly bat, a rusty chair
A fat cat, a mouldy pear

Spin, spin with a spoon
Let a fire roar up to the moon

A smell of a dog, a wolf's tail
A leg of a frog, the shell of a snail
A tattered pan, a rotten pie
A squashed can, a spotty tie

Spin, spin with a spoon
Let a fire roar up to the moon

Hairy feet, a broken table
A comfy seat, a messy stable
A popped ball, a child's cry
A small hall, a witch's lie

This a spell for a week
To make you beautiful
But don't forget
You have a witch's nose.

Charlotte Karpow (11)
Thorpe Willoughby CP School

Macbeth

M acbeth killed the king
A nd got very upset
C ouldn't pull himself together
B ad he had been
E ven Lady Macbeth couldn't calm him
T empted he was, but now he was not
H e was ashamed over what he had done.

Sean Greenwood (10)
Thorpe Willoughby CP School

The Sailing Boat

My grandad has a sailing boat
On the windowsill,
I imagined I went sailing on it
With my friend, old Bill.

I imagined on that day I would
Sail around the world,
I would go to all the continents
And the boot with its rim curved.

My grandad would say
'When I was a lad, I went for a trip on this boat,
I caught lots of fish, and fell into a river
I was pushed in by the horns of a goat.'

'The boat is fantastic,' I said, with a smile
'I wish I was like you, I would find lots of bones,
Then I would find a pirate's ship
Just like Sir Indiana Jones.'

'Time for bed, little one, enough stories for you,
You can go fast to sleep in a flight,
You can sail on our boat around in your dream
Only don't make a peep.Goodnight.'

Sara Thompson (9)
Thorpe Willoughby CP School

Stars

Millions of glitter balls in the sky,
Sources of light that caught my eye.

Glistening bright on a blanket of blue,
Hundreds of years old but shining like new.

The Plough, Orion and Great Bear,
I always love to stop and stare.

Silver sparkles miles away,
Visible at night, but not in the day.

Aimée Schofield (10)
Thorpe Willoughby CP School

Weather

The sun is so bright,
And the clouds are so
Grey,
When they mix together,
It is thunder every day.

Fog is so misty it is,
So dark and grey,
It can't go away,
Because it stays with you,
All the day.

When the sun is out, the air
Is so fresh,
And the cool wind you can
Hear and touch.

I love the snow, it is so cool,
And my friend, Mary
Throws snowballs at everyone.

Lora Barratt
Thorpe Willoughby CP School

Knight

An iron man
A metal soldier
An old Englishman
A castle guard
A king's warrior
A great spear-thrower
A sword-player
A shining being
An armoured human
A beast-slayer.

Steven Flanagan (10)
Thorpe Willoughby CP School

Storm Snow-Rain

Storm snow-rain
All of these can be
You
When sizzling sun
Burns my bun
Storm snow-rain
All of these can be
You
Cool, refreshing rain
Is always insane
Storm snow-rain
All of these can be
You
Snowflakes fall
A lightning storm.

Laura Hill (9)
Thorpe Willoughby CP School

Kennings

A snowball season
A cold time of year
A sledging time
A wet season
A freezing time
Christmas time
Time for animals to hibernate
A snowy season
A last season
A coldest season.

Tom Wales (9)
Thorpe Willoughby CP School

A Witch's Spell

All: double trouble, fizz, whizz
Trouble in a pot.

Witch 1: a white lie, a nasty bump
Witch 2: pumpkin pie, a bruised lump.
Witch 3: a smelly boot, a garden snail
Witch 1: a horn's toot, a fish scale.

All: double trouble, fizz, whizz
Trouble in a pot.

Witch 2: a surprised child's wow, lava so hot
Witch 3: a newly-born cow, a tiny baby's cot.
Witch 1: a gas-filled spark, a tail of a dog
Witch 2: a singing lark, a rotten log.

All: double trouble, fizz, whizz
Trouble in a pot.

Witch 3: a toxic smell, a lamb's baa
Witch 1: water from a well, an opera singer's la.
Witch 2: a fat mouse, a head louse
Witch 3: a ping, a pong, a bing, a bong.

All: double trouble, fizz, whizz
Trouble in a pot.

All: this is a spell of pure evil,
for a weapon so lethal.

Nadia Smith (10)
Thorpe Willoughby CP School

If I Were . . .

If I were a dog I would be
A fluffy Labrador puppy
I would play all day
Then hide away.

If I were a cat I would be
A fluffy tabby kitten
I would play with my tinkle ball
And get strokes and pats from all.

If I were a tree
I would be a hollow one
For insects and bugs
I would keep them warm and snug.

If I were a teacher
I wouldn't be strict
I would like to teach art
But ICT is pretty smart.

If I were a wild animal
I would be a leopard
I couldn't change my spots
But I wouldn't be a cheetah.

If I were a fairy I could
Fly so high
I would fly to the moon on a bee
But I prefer to just be me.

Stacey Nix (11)
Thorpe Willoughby CP School

What Is?

What is the sun?
It is a large ball of fire that smiles to you
but you can't see it.

Where does the sky begin?
Over the hills and far away.

Where does time go?
Underwater and back up again to start afresh.

What is inside a hill?
A large bunch of people trying to get out.

Is life a dream?
Sometimes it is a dream because you get to do
some wonderful things in life.

How does a window see?
There is a large person inside with a magnifying
glass waiting to see.

What is in a waterfall?
Baby creatures that fall in the water and scream.

How does wind blow?
With a big hiss and a loud blow.

Why do we dream?
To have a better life in future.

What is sand?
Baby spots painted yellow.

What is the sky?
A large shark that covers the entire world.

Why do stars shine?
So your dead relatives can look after you.

Aimee Barratt (11)
Thorpe Willoughby CP School

Witch's Spell

Bang bang, pip pop,
Make potions in our greasy pot.

A teacher's toe, the mind of a pest,
A little devil, a sweaty vest,
An alligator's tooth, a lion's roar,
A bear's big foot, a tiger's claw.

Bang bang, pip pop,
Make potions in our greasy pot.

A tongue of a parent, a stinging bee,
The foot of a brother, a dog's flea,
A heart of a pig, a wing of a bat,
The spit of a camel, a cow's fat.

Bang bang, pip pop,
Make potions in our greasy pot.

Aaron Williams (10)
Thorpe Willoughby CP School

Thunder And Lightning

A howling werewolf
A flash of striking light
A gloomy sky
Some howling trees
Careless rain
Bashing branches
What am I?

Victoria Amos (9)
Thorpe Willoughby CP School

Silly Seasons

On the ground in spring there
Are lots of funny flower buds
That look as though they should
Be around a tower in a storybook.

Silly starry seasons
Jolly jockey seasons
Cold crazy seasons
Lazy lolly seasons
Seasons
Seasons
Seasons.

The sky in summer is a yellow
Basketball that shines, as though
It's never going to fall.

Silly starry seasons . . .

On the trees in autumn there are
Multicoloured leaves that blow
To faraway places and never seem
To leave.

Silly starry seasons . . .

On the floor in winter is a cold fur
Coat that feels like a boat on the
Sea.

Silly starry seasons . . .

I like all the different seasons
They always are such fun, they
Go round and round like a
Merry-go-round that's never going to
Stop.

Silly starry seasons . . .

Bethany Wadlow (9)
Thorpe Willoughby CP School

Snappy Seasons

The season is spring,
It's scattered with dew,
The sun came out,
And the flowers they grew.

The season is summer,
I feel a sense of delight,
I feel a tingle in my bones,
Because the sun is shining bright.

The season is autumn,
It's sometimes very mild,
But I hope in the afternoon,
The wind turns it wild.

The season is winter,
It is very snowy,
But in the heart of the wind,
It is very blowy.

So after all those seasons,
I think you'll agree,
We'd occasionally stay inside,
And let the weather be.

Sian McEvoy (8)
Thorpe Willoughby CP School

Thunder And Lightning

The lightning and thunder makes me wonder
The lightning is frightening
The thunder goes under
The lightning is brightening.

The thunder roaring and pouring
When you are inside, yawning
Lightning flashing and flowing
And the wind stops blowing.

Craig May (8)
Thorpe Willoughby CP School

Mixed-Up Tewahre (Weather)

A howling wind
A mysterious fog
A blinding sun
A pelting snow
A freezing ice
A deep dark puddle
A sweltering fire
A tip-tapping of rain
A round warm sun
An evil wet rain
A very solid ice
A steaming fire
A damp puddle
A roaring wind
A deep flood
A fierce tornado.

Lauren Golton (9)
Thorpe Willoughby CP School

Thunder And Lightning

A drizzling sky
A wet floor
A flash of light
A grey sky
A near sound
A bet to stop
A crack in the sky
A quick flash
A never-stopping thing
A grey cloud
A loud bang.

Rebecca Cram (9)
Thorpe Willoughby CP School

Weather

When it's icy I slide around
I like sliding, it is fun
When I step in the ice, I like the sound
And sometimes I have to stay in.

When it snows we make a snowman
And sometimes we have a big snowball fight
Then I get a snowball in my face and it goes bang
My team always wins.

I like it the most when it is bright
Because I know the sun is up
As morning and night are still light
With my mum saying, 'Make that your last cup.'

Rain and showers come and go
Making everything cold and wet
But, thank God, it doesn't snow
As pneumonia we might get.

Alex Parkin (9)
Thorpe Willoughby CP School

What Is It?

A white fluffy sheep,
A rain machine,
A sea absorber,
A piece of cotton wool,
A sun and sky blocker,
A vapour floater,
A state of gloom,
A mass of tiny water-drops,
A snow-carrier,
A floating smoke.

Joshua Humphrey-Shepherd (9)
Thorpe Willoughby CP School

Weather

Snow is white,
Sun is bright,
Snow is cold,
Sun is light.

Snow you can feel,
Sun you see,
Wind that can blow,
Fun in the snow.

Howling wind,
Pelting rain,
Rushing wind,
Hitting windowpane.

Nicholas Bingham (9)
Thorpe Willoughby CP School

Snow

A cold-giver,
A little shiver,
A blizzard-maker,
A coat-toucher,
A worry-maker.

A thing that kids love,
And play with all day,
They have snowball fights,
And build different things in different ways.

But then the sun comes out and dries it all up,
So the sun has spoilt all the children's fun.

Stephanie Freer (8)
Thorpe Willoughby CP School

Wild Wind

A cold-giver
A little shiver
A howling thing that's
hard to see.

It creeps and crawls down your
spine and only comes in winter.

A cold-giver
A little shiver
A howling thing that's
hard to see.

You may be able to feel it
You may be able to hear it
But you can't see it.

A cold-giver
A little shiver
A howling thing that's
hard to see.

It comes in different sizes
It comes in different shapes
It sometimes comes in whirlwinds
Round and round they twirl.

A cold-giver
A little shiver
A howling thing that's
hard to see.

My coat and hat shall keep
me warm
So wild, whirling winds won't
come my way.

Maggie Hymes (9)
Thorpe Willoughby CP School

Weather

I like rain
I can sing in the rain
It goes on my window
And I make it fun by playing a game

The sun comes out
Everyone goes out to play
Then we will play
Play more and you will be happy

The stormy weather
A tiny blast, a gigantic tornado
And a roaring whirlwind
A big twister

When the snow falls
A frozen vapour, a little snowball
A place of snow
That's what snow can do

The misty weather
A fog, a haze, and
A big smog
A little drizzle

When it is boiling
It is a ray from the sun
When it is boiling
It is really hot

When it is cold
It is a leak from
Your nose
That's why I like the cold

When it hails
It's like a big, tough nail
A fall of ice
A shower too, but made of ice.

Matthew Wain (9)
Thorpe Willoughby CP School

Weather Discovery

A light start,
A petrifying noise,
A sweltering heat,
A jungle storm,
A dampening river,
A blinding mist,
A howling draught,
A sea of dust,
A dark end.

Emily Burton (9)
Thorpe Willoughby CP School

What We Do!

Fridge-raider
Ball-stopper
Burger-destroyer
Bullseye-archer
Babe-magnet
Food-stuffer
Corkie-smasher
Toy-breaker
Man U-fanatic
Lord Of The Rings-frantic
Football-fiend
Animal-lover
Robot Wars-watcher
School-hater

Jono Trowsdale (9) & William Ashton (10)
West Heslerton CE Primary School

Us

PlayStation-player
Chicken-destroyer!
Plan-plotter
Race-runners
Snowboarding-supreme
Skating-stinker
Orc-thrasher
Maths-madness
School-superstars
Food! - Magic
Child-terror
Computer-crasher

Matthew Marucci (9) & Daniel Burns (11)
West Heslerton CE Primary School

What We Do

Joy-rider
School-hater
Friend-loser
Seat-slumper
Mobile phone-mad
Book-binder
Food-aholic
Pudding-muncher
Embarrassing mum-owner
TV-square eyes
Animal-lover.

Hannah Clay (11) & Louise Milner
West Heslerton CE Primary School

What Us Kids Are Like

Alarm-destroyers
Food-munchers
Sport-lovers
Sweet-chompers
Book-worms
Piano-players
School-haters
Chatter-boxes
Teddy-fans
Telly-addicts
Baby brother-dislikers.

Jenny Hyde (9) Sara Parker (9)
West Heslerton CE Primary School

About Me!

Road-slasher
Clothes-puncher
Football-smasher
Rugby-player
Breakfast-cruncher
BMX-rider
Bike-breaker
PS2-lover
Burger-basher
Chip-cracker
Dare-devil
Pogo-puncher

Thomas Parsons (10) & Jake Handley
West Heslerton CE Primary School

My Poem

Chocolate-licker
Duvet-snatcher
Bed-lover
Breakfast-snatcher
Family-lover
Brother-lover
Alarm-crusher
Mum-carer
Film-watcher
Soap-destroyer
Bath-hater
Child-supporter

Josephine Watson (10) & Leanne Pickering (10)
West Heslerton CE Primary School

My Sandwich

Bread goes crunch and also goes crackle.
Lettuce goes crunch and is hard to tackle.
Cheese makes you and a friend go 'Ugh!'
And chicken makes puppies go 'Woof' or 'Grrr!'
Tuna makes cats or kittens go 'miaow.'
You need to eat beef and it comes from a cow.
Meat from a pig, you gulp it down and it's called pork.
This is the sandwich that I made in York!

Charlie Ward (11)
West Heslerton CE Primary School